ADVERTISING AND SOCIALISM

By the same author

The Consumer in the Soviet Economy

ADVERTISING AND SOCIALISM

The Nature and Extent of Consumer Advertising in the Soviet Union, Poland, Hungary and Yugoslavia

Philip Hanson

International Arts and Sciences Press, Inc.
White Plains, New York

Published in Great Britain by The Macmillan Press Ltd.

First U.S. edition published in 1974 by
International Arts and Sciences Press, Inc.
901 North Broadway, White Plains, New York 10603

Library of Congress Catalog Card Number: 73-92711

International Standard Book Number: 0-87332-053-0

Printed in Great Britain

Contents

Preface

The idea of making a study of advertising in socialist countries was originally suggested to me by Mr Harold Lind of the (British) Advertising Association. It seemed an intrinsically interesting subject, as well as a natural extension of work I had done earlier on the consumer sector of the Soviet economy. I had doubts, though, about whether there was really much advertising to investigate, at least in the Comecon countries. A preliminary check suggested that there was, after all, a tiny but growing volume of consumer advertising even in countries such as the Soviet Union, which had detailed central planning, and substantially more in the recently decentralised Hungarian economy and pre-invasion Czechoslovakia. And of course, outside the Soviet orbit there was the relatively market-oriented and Westernised Yugoslav economy. This suggested that there were after all some interesting questions to answer: Why did an administrative economy like the Soviet one have any domestic consumer advertising at all, and why was it, apparently, growing? What did evidence from Hungary and Yugoslavia suggest about the scale and functions of advertising in more decentralised socialist economies?

The bulk of the research was done in 1970 and 1971, with the assistance of a research grant from the Advertising Association, and written up in 1971—2. I looked first at the Soviet situation and then at that in Poland, Hungary and Yugoslavia. The reasons for this choice of countries are explained in the Introduction. In the case of the Soviet Union this study is based on a reading of the rapidly-growing Soviet literature on marketing and a series of interviews with Soviet marketing people in the summer of 1970. In the case of the East European countries I have relied more heavily on interviews, conducted in 1971, and have not attempted to survey the very large marketing literature of these three countries. In general, statements made in this book about 'the present' or 'the recent' past should be understood as referring to late 1970 in the case of the USSR, and mid-1971 in the case of Poland, Hungary and Yugoslavia. I have however added some comments, mainly in footnotes, on developments through 1972, where this seemed particularly desirable. On the whole there do not seem to have been significant changes in the marketing environments of these countries since the interviews were carried out. One must however note some tightening-up on excessive 'decadence' in public display in Yugoslavia, to which I have referred in a footnote in Chapter 7, and the apparently modest changes introduced at the Hungarian Socialist Workers' Party Central Committee meeting of December 1972. It is possible that the latter may come in time to be seen as the beginning of a process of re-centralisation in Hungary; but at the time of writing (January 1973) the prospects of the Hungarian New Economic Mechanism still seem, to an outsider, fairly open.

This study was originally published (in 1971 and 1972) as two separate monographs, dealing with the Soviet Union and Eastern Europe separately, in the Advertising Association's 'Research Studies in Advertising' series. I have made a number of changes in order to turn them into one coherent whole, and some additions and amendments to take account of some more recent information.

I am indebted to a large number of people for assistance in carrying out this study. The Advertising Association not only gave financial support for the research but provided me with opportunities to discuss problems and findings with advertising practitioners and others who know far more than I do about the business of advertising and marketing in general. I am especially indebted to Mr Harold Lind of the Advertising Association for his extremely helpful advice and comments throughout this study.

Many other people generously shared their knowledge of Soviet and East European marketing with me, providing me variously with contacts, statistical data, information on sources and problems of data, and information and insight into the functioning of advertising in the Soviet Union and Eastern Europe. I should like to express my thanks to all of them.

In the UK I was considerably helped by Mr Barry Douthwaite of Gillette Industries Ltd, Mr Alfred Dubs of J. Walter Thompson, Mr Leopold Friedman of the Owen Organisation, Mr Lex Hornsby of Lex Hornsby Associates, Mr Andrew Knee of Reckitt and Colman Ltd and Mr Robert S. Leaf of Marsteller International; and in Geneva by Mr J. R.Mikton of UNCTAD/GATT.

In the Soviet Union Professor Ya. Zasurskii and the directors and members of staff of the Soviet advertising organisations, Soyuztorgreklama, Rostorgreklama and Ukrtorgreklama, and of the Mezhduvedomstvennyi Sovet po Reklame were most generous in giving time to answering my questions and discussing the functions of advertising in the USSR.

I am most grateful to all the East European marketing specialists who were so kind as to spend a great deal of time with me, answering numerous and detailed questions and giving me the benefit of their knowledge of East European marketing and their insights into causal relationships: in Warsaw Mr Edward Lehwark of the Ministry of Internal Trade, Mr Miechyslaw Muszkowski of COK Reclama, Dr Edmund Paszkowiak, Mr Jan Plociniak and Mr Krzysztof Sokolik of AGPOL, Mr Jan Szalowski of the Higher School of Planning and Statistics and Dr Tadeusz Sztucki of the Institute of Internal Trade; in Budapest Dr Pal Kurthy of the University of Economics and the Ministry of Foreign Trade, Professor Endre Megyuri of the University of Economics, Dr Karoly Ravasz, Director of Hungexpo, Dr Laszlo Szabo, Managing Director of the Hungarian Institute for Market Research, Dr Anna Sandor of the Centre for Afro-Asian Research of the Hungarian Academy of Sciences and Mr Endre Zsigmundi, Director of Magyar Hirdeto; in Zagreb by Professor Fedor Rocco, Director of ZIT, Mr Mihovil Skobe, Mrs Tudor and Mr Mutic of OZEHA.

My colleague, Mr Geoffrey Barker, read a preliminary draft of the Soviet monograph and made many valuable comments on it.

I doubt if any of the people who helped in these various ways will agree with all my interpretations and conclusions. I hope, however, that the Soviet and East European specialists, in particular, while not necessarily agreeing with all my conclusions, will recognise in what follows an attempt at a fair and accurate survey of the subject.

1 Introduction: Advertising, Soviet-type economies and economic systems

Advertising and socialism

Socialists have never liked the advertising industry. There must be many people working in advertising in the West who would consider themselves to be socialists; but this does not seem to have helped in any ideological *rapprochement*.

According to the 'official' Marxist—Leninist tradition represented by modern Soviet doctrine, advertising in the West is part of the mechanism of exploitation in present-day capitalist societies. Soviet writers point to the substantial margin between production and transport costs on the one hand and final prices, especially of consumer goods, on the other in the industrialised West. They argue that distributive margins, which are in general substantially higher than in communist countries, include a large component of surplus value extracted both in overt profits and in inflated managerial salaries and expenses. Part of this accrues directly to the advertising industry. In addition advertising, like other forms of marketing, fosters monopoly power and monopoly profit, thus assisting the extraction of surplus value by producers. From the point of view of economic efficiency, much of Western marketing activity is considered in Soviet doctrine to be a wasteful use of resources, adding nothing to real output and keeping a substantial part of the labour force 'non-productively' employed.

In the West criticism of advertising, whether reformist or radical, tends to put more emphasis on its alleged social and cultural effects: it diverts our energies from increased leisure or a better provision of public services to the production and

1

consumption of trivial consumer goods we do not really want; it promotes greedy and philistine attitudes generally; or it is part of an overall process of manipulation and control of people in advanced industrial societies.

Common to most social criticisms of advertising is the view that a socialist system would, or could, reduce or eliminate the ill effects imputed to the advertising industry. It is interesting to find, therefore, that commercial advertising exists and is increasing in the USSR and Eastern Europe. Of course, there are many hypothetical socialisms, and many socialists would consider these countries either to be not socialist at all or to be examples of socialism in a seriously flawed form — the difference between these two views is merely definitional. At all events these are countries with predominant public ownership of productive resources; evidence about the extent to which they use commercial advertising and the purposes to which they put it should throw some light on the relationship between advertising and socialised ownership. One cannot, however, make any grandiose claims for this evidence. It cannot either exonerate or condemn Western advertising expenditure in general, and on some of the issues it sheds little light. What it can do is to identify some of the institutional arrangements that encourage advertising and some that do not. It helps to clarify the relationship between socialised ownership of resources and marketing activity, and it shows (if it is not already obvious) the futility of attacking or defending the advertising industry without taking a definite view about the overall system of resource allocation that one prefers.

The aims of this book are to describe the present organisation and recent development of advertising in some of these countries; to try to measure the size and recent growth rates of their advertising expenditure and compare it to that of the UK, and to assess the purposes that their advertising serves. My work has been concerned mainly with advertising of consumer goods on domestic markets and not with the advertising of these countries on foreign markets. Industrial marketing is discussed only in passing. In the highly centralised systems (the USSR and Poland, in the present study), central allocation of producer goods almost eliminates the need for industrial marketing. In Hungary and Yugoslavia it is more significant, and some reference is made to it in discussing those countries. The advertising of foreign consumer goods, particularly Western goods, on Soviet and East Europe markets is considered here both as a component in their total domestic advertising and as an influence on the marketing of domestically produced goods. I have not, however, tried to cover the subject of Western export marketing in these countries from the Western exporter's point of view.

The countries that I have studied in some detail are the USSR, Poland, Hungary and Yugoslavia. This choice, and the amount of attention given to each of the four, requires some explanation. There were two reasons for beginning with the USSR. In the first place, mere expediency: the Soviet Union is the country of which I have made a specialised study in the past; I therefore know more about it. Secondly, it is in several ways a logical starting-point. The Soviet economic system is the classic working example of a state-owned and centrally planned economy. It was for a considerable time the model for the other Comecon countries and, for a much briefer period, for Yugoslavia. It is true that differences between the economic management systems of the Comecon countries are now greater than they were in the late 1950s. Nonetheless, in most of the Comecon countries planning and control still have what are generally thought to be key basic features in common with the USSR. The only exception is Hungary, which in 1968 shifted to a substantially decentralised New Economic Mechanism which continues with minor modifications up to the time of writing (January 1973).

I have therefore started with Soviet advertising and given it a more detailed and extensive treatment than that of the other three countries. The logic of this is that the assessment of advertising in the Soviet economy provides a bench-mark. It shows why even in a highly centralised system commercial advertising has begun to have a role of some significance; on the other hand it shows why there are, at the same time, severe limits to that role in such a system. As far as the importance of advertising is concerned, however, the weight given here to the Soviet Union is excessive. Hungarian and

Yugoslav advertising are much more developed, yet they are given a more superficial treatment. The first part of this study, in other words, uses a steamhammer to crack a nut; the second part, unfortunately, uses a lot less power on a somewhat larger nut. All the same, if the development of Soviet advertising is still embryonic and its future direction uncertain, it has gone far enough to be more than a minor curiosity, and it does serve as an introduction to developments in more decentralised socialist economies.

Of the East European countries, Poland, Hungary and Yugoslavia are considered here. These were the countries for which it seemed, from preliminary correspondence, that information was most readily available. They provide a spectrum of economic management systems. The Polish economy is, very broadly, still a centralised, Soviet-type system, though its marketing environment differs in several ways from that of the USSR. The Hungarian and Yugoslav economies, on the other hand, can both be loosely described as 'market socialist' systems, but with considerable differences (in 1970—1) in methods and degree of central control and, particularly, in openness to Western trade and marketing. Thus the marketing environment is more or less of a 'Soviet' kind in Poland, more nearly 'Western' in Yugoslavia; while in Hungary it has been in a state of rapid evolution since the introduction of the New Economic Mechanism in 1968.

Of the East European countries not studied here, the DDR (East Germany) seems the most serious omission. It has the highest per capita GNP and personal real income levels of all communist countries and an economic management system which, though broadly speaking 'centralised', is more sophisticated than that of the Soviet Union and has certain elements of decentralised decision-making, absent in the USSR, which might be expected to encourage marketing activity. For Czechoslovakia, however, the Comecon country with the next highest per capita income level, I have been able to refer to the results of an earlier Western study of advertising and marketing expenditure in 1967. Altogether, the material assembled in this study provides evidence on the scale and functions of commercial consumer advertising in socialist economies with quite widely differing income levels and both with and without detailed central allocation of goods.

The rest of this introductory chapter is devoted to conceptual ground-clearing. I shall set out some possible hypotheses, first about the role of advertising in a Soviet-type economy, and secondly about the influences on the volume of advertising in any economic system.

What is meant here by the phrase 'Soviet-type economy' is a national economy in which land and productive capital are predominantly state-owned and resource allocation is predominantly by administrative control in accordance with a single central plan. The basic production units, whether factories, farms, construction organisations, shipping lines or basic units in other fields of activity, are given detailed instructions abut the level, composition, pricing and allocation of their output by a superior authority (for instance, a branch ministry) which is itself required to carry out part of an overall national plan. Defined in these fairly broad terms, the description 'Soviet-type economy' can still be applied to all the socialist countries of Eastern Europe, despite some variations in their arrangements, with two clear exceptions: Hungary and Yugoslavia.

In these two countries the normal arrangement now is for enterprises not to receive output and other plan instructions but to make their own decisions on the basis of profit-linked incentives and within a framework of centrally determined rules of the game, including (particularly in Hungary) many price controls. The Hungarian and Yugoslav economic systems therefore, while retaining (in different forms) socialised ownership and control, have in recent years been clearly outside the 'Soviet-type' or 'Administrative' category.

Individual features of the various national planning and management systems, in so far as they are relevant to the marketing environment, are described in chapters 2, 5 and 6 below.

Possible functions of advertising in the Soviet-type economy
Some obvious and trivial propositions about the nature of commercial advertising in the West will help us to understand

the actual or possible functions of advertising in a Soviet-type economy. To begin with, advertising aims to sell goods or services. It is paid for by producers and distributors who have stocks or supply capacity, an incentive to sell and a belief that advertising will help sales.

Just what advertising does do for the sale of goods is not at all clear; hence the very large scope for attacking and defending it, and generally earning royalties for eloquence on the subject. What is clear in Western industrial society is that there are people who normally have a strong interest in raising or at least maintaining the sales of various things, and hence in some form of marketing. They are, roughly, the senior managers and less directly the shareholders of private firms.[1]

Also, it is widely, though vaguely, agreed that the appearance of average consumption levels of the kind now found in Western Europe and — from an earlier date — in North America makes consumer demand more a matter of individual discretion, or indiscretion, than before. There are more alternative things available to spend one's money on, and a greater proportion of them are things one could physically do without. So the scope for sellers to influence buyers' behaviour, at least in retail markets, by some form of advertising has grown.[2]

It is not so obvious how advertising fits into an economy of the Soviet type. For those who preach some sort of convergence theory there is no problem: all modern industrial societies are doomed to become more and more alike. But to most Westerners at all familiar with the Soviet system the differences at present with respect to marketing seem significant and durable. The very term 'marketing' is a little out of place in an economic system where so many functions assigned in the West to the market are performed by

[1] Modern contributions to the theory of the private-enterprise firm by Baumol, Downie, Marris, Penrose and others tend to give more prominence to the goal of increasing sales over time than does neo-classical theory, and to relate this to modern management career incentives in large companies. See particularly Robin Marris, *The Economic Theory of Managerial Capitalism* (Macmillan, 1963).
[2] See George Katona, *The Mass Consumption Society* (McGraw-Hill, 1964), as well as Galbraith.

centralised allocation. Associated with this are price control and a tendency to repressed inflation, i.e. shortages and sellers' markets. The nearest traditional Russian term to 'marketing' is *'sbyt'*, which means simply 'disposal' (of output). Differences of system apart, there is also the question of relative consumption levels. How much scope is there for consumer advertising at present Soviet consumption levels?

The obvious question to ask, then, is who has an incentive to advertise in the Soviet economy? As a guide to subsequent discussion there are several possible answers to this.

First, it may be argued that the leadership and central planners are fundamentally the initiators and controllers of advertising. Soviet writers on advertising stress that in a 'socialist' (i.e. Soviet-type) economy basic production decisions are centralised and marketing decisions are not left to those who in a private-enterprise economy have a material interest in selling more. This is claimed to be a great advantage. Consumer advertising can be developed and consumer demand stimulated only so far and in such directions as is rational or desirable. Central planning of the growth of private consumption can reflect people's true wants rather than the particular interests of private sellers.[3]

What does this mean? We could interpret it to mean that the central planners have read Galbraith and are trying to give a higher priority to public goods, leisure or, say, gifts to underdeveloped countries by eliminating the 'dependence effect' or 'revised sequence'. Thinking of this sort was embodied to some extent in the 'Khrushchev' consumption targets for the achievement of full communism by 1980. If the (Khrushchev) 'rational consumption norms' which were associated with the consumer-goods output targets for 1980 represented a vision of abundance, it was a puritan vision, e.g. with respect to private cars. At that time, before the Fiat deal, widespread ownership of private cars was still ruled out.

---

[3] The books of Bekleshov, Bekleshov and Voronov, and Degtyarev and Kornilov (see appendix A) all put great emphasis on this, before going on to explain how useful and effective capitalist advertising techniques can be in socialism.

It was considered more 'rational' to have a national car-rental pool.[4]

It is not clear how rational comsumption levels are determined, however. Broadly, the official Soviet goal seems in practice to be to catch up with US levels. This rather restricts the application of Galbraithian limits to Soviet consumer-goods production. For the time being, the desirability of raising consumption levels indefinitely is taken for granted. Medium-term (five-year) and longer-run Soviet plans are currently said to be based on a choice of alternative plan variants, of which the minimum variant (from the point of view of consumption) must at least entail no fall in average consumption levels.[5] The Soviet literature, moreover, normally asserts not only that consumption levels should be raised, but that people's 'wants' should also be increased. This probably means that if consumer advertising is needed to introduce products new in the USSR but established in the USA, or to raise consumption levels of old products to US levels, it will be developed as a matter of national policy. However, imitation of Western consumption patterns need not be slavish. A consumption level is a highly aggregated thing, and there are various ways of raising it. So if, for example, it is easier to improve the Soviet diet by increasing the Soviet fishing fleet and catching more fish than by increasing the output of meat from Soviet agriculture, or if it is considered to be socially preferable to have launderettes instead of large stocks of under-utilised, privately owned washing machines, advertising can be used to mould demand in these particular directions — if possible. So one interpretation could be that top-level policy controls advertising with the long-run macroeconomic aim of catching up and surpassing US consumption levels, though the detail of this broad policy may be modified by considerations of expediency and social policy.

Secondly, it may be argued that, in some relevant respects,

---

[4] For a discussion of the rational norms, see the appendix to chapter 4.
[5] (4), p. 44. (In the Introduction and in Part I, numbers in round brackets in the footnotes refer to the numbered books and articles in the bibliography of Soviet works (appendix A). Factual information on Soviet advertising given without footnotes in the text is derived from interviews.)

the basic decision-making unit in the Soviet economy is the sector ministry or its administrative subdivision, the *glavk*, which is responsible for a branch within the sector managed by the ministry.[6] Ministries and *glavki* deal with one another and with central authorities through administrative channels rather than market relationships, but they are production-based interest groups with some influence on central decisions and some discretion in implementing them. In so far as their output is marketed rather than administratively allocated, they operate as product monopolies subject to price control. There is some evidence of ministries and *glavki* developing marketing activities, including advertising, and it is worth considering how far they are the initiators of advertising expenditure, and what their interest in advertising is.

If, in a Soviet-type economy, advertising decisions are made at a national-economy or sector level, or both, is there no competitive brand advertising? Soviet writers often claim that the Soviet system can avoid costly but socially un-rewarding advertising undertaken by Western industries which have inter-firm competition. This argument is reminiscent of the criticism by Kaldor and others of 'defensive' advertising expenditure and of the reports of the Prices and Incomes Board on detergents and confectionery production. The counter-argument in these cases has been that this advertising expenditure is an unavoidable result of product competition in certain conditions and that product competition offers more than offsetting advantages.[7] Can we learn anything about this from Soviet experience? Certainly Soviet management at enterprise level is in some respects motivated to restrict targets in order to obtain bonuses for

[6] (11); (33). There has been a shift in emphasis in the past two years or so from the development of enterprise autonomy to the development of ministry, devision or combine autonomy. This is partly but not wholly a 'centralist' reaction, and autonomy is hardly very great so far even at these levels, but it does seem a more realistic line of development. It has lately been taken further. The decree of April 1973 on industrial associations outlines a planned re-organisation of Soviet industry which is designed to shift a considerable amount of decision-making to new sub-branch management bodies: national and republic industrial associations.

[7] See the article by Adrian Cadbury in the *Advertising Quarterly* (Summer 1969).

plan fulfilment more easily,[8] so that we might not expect Soviet enterprises to have an interest in marketing. One question, clearly, is how far Soviet production does in practice avoid inter-firm competition in marketing. Another question is what the net advantages are, in so far as it does.

A third view would be that advertising has only a minor and insignificant role in the Soviet-type economy. The only advertising that might be attempted would be to get rid of stocks of some very obsolete, sub-standard or otherwise undesirable item. Apart from that, market relationships are not important enough for marketing expenditure to be incurred. In other words, the only role of advertising must be to remedy occasional gross errors.

There are several arguments in favour of this view. In the first place, it is true that private per capita consumption levels are still relatively low — of the order of half of UK levels[9] — and 'discretionary' expenditure is limited. Admittedly discretionary consumer expenditure is hard to define in Soviet circumstances. The proportion of total private expenditure that goes on in housing is low, probably about 5 per cent. But the proportion that goes on food is still relatively large — about 45 per cent.[10]

Most important is the prevalence of shortages and sellers' markets at existing, controlled prices. Peasant markets and black markets apart, the position in consumer markets is one of approximate price control without a completely successful control of total disposable money incomes, and hence repressed inflation. The excess of peasant-market over state retail prices for some food items; the very high black market prices for a number of things, e.g. Western clothing; the waiting list for cars and some other durables, and the opinion of Soviet economists that a large part of personal savings is merely frustrated spending-money that failed to be spent because the would-be purchasers could not find the goods they wanted — all these things give some indication of the

[8] (33).
[9] P. Hanson, *The Consumer in the Soviet Economy* (Macmillan, 1968), chapter 4.
[10] ibid.

scale of these shortages. (The merit of Soviet price control, of course, is that the cost of living changes relatively little over time.[11]) The extent of shortages in producer goods markets is harder to assess. It may be exaggerated by the system of finance and material allocation, which induces enterprises and ministries to put in high bids for supplies of materials and equipment.

In general, sellers' markets prevail, and marketing is correspondingly underdeveloped. In this situation distributors are apt to accept even unwanted supplies from producers in order to maintain good relations with them. It follows from this that the burden of marketing those items that do not 'sell themselves' at existing prices falls largely on the distributive system. Advertising in general remains, on this view, a minor phenomenon for which the economic system in general provides little encouragement. It will be used mainly by distributors rather than producers. Official attempts to foster it will be simply a misguided attempt to emulate the West. If we find that Soviet advertising expenditure is relatively very small, not increasing fast, and incurred almost exclusively by distributors, that would be evidence favouring this interpretation.

Finally, it might be suggested that the socialist economies are evolving towards a blend of market and plan which will be more or less indistinguishable from other advanced economies — a convergence to a new industrial state in which differences in resource-ownership are merely a formality, and control and decision-making are organised and motivated in much the same way as in modern Western economies. If this were so, commercial advertising, among other things, would now be developing towards current Western functions and organisation. Increasingly, producers as well as distributors,

[11] It is often said, both by Western and Soviet sources, that there has been some 'concealed open inflation', as opposed to plain repressed inflation, in the Soviet Union in the 1960s, through the disappearance of cheaper varieties of products, the introduction of new products at higher prices and so on, which are not properly allowed for by the official retail price index. See particularly (7), p. 133. This is almost certainly correct, but I doubt if a corrected index would show more than a very slow rate of increase by Western European or North American standards.

and enterprises and combines as well as ministries, would find advertising useful. There would be some real decentralisation of economic decision-making and it would be associated with the appearance of marketing orientation at enterprise and combine levels. Managers of production units would increasingly be interested in enlarging the sales of products to which their current equipment and know-how in some degree committed them, and also in increasing profits by moving, if necessary with considerable selling costs, into substantially new markets on their own initiative. This is indeed the case in Hungary and Yugoslavia, which are no longer Soviet-type, administrative economies, but it is not the case elsewhere.

These possible functions for advertising in the Soviet-type economy are not all mutually exclusive. But if there is much substance in the idea that Soviet economic reform is part of a process of East—West convergence, Soviet and East European advertising will be developing a Western character, being made at enterprise, combine or ministry level by producers as well as distributors and with expenditure rising towards Western levels. (After all, it hardly looks as if Western marketing is converging towards traditional Soviet practice.) If there really is a process of convergence going on in this sphere, both Soviet-style direction of advertising by central planners and the constraint of sellers' markets on the level of Soviet and Eastern European expenditure on advertising would be of dwindling importance.

Advertising and economic systems
The other basic question I have in mind in looking at Soviet and Eastern European advertising is: what can it tell us about the nature and functions of advertising in any economy? For advertising, as for other things, the Soviet and East European economies provide a sort of crude laboratory test which may help us to understand our own economic system better.

What determines the volume of advertising in any economy? The following propositions do not constitute a respectable scientific hypothesis; more precise definitions and quantifiable relationships would be needed to test them. They are offered, in the absence of data with which we could test more precise versions, merely as an aid to reflection on what data we have.

If advertising is defined as the International Advertising Association has defined it, to include display and other (technical, financial, small advertisments) advertising in the press, cinema, radio, television, by outdoor signs and by mail, plus commercial exhibitions, shop-window displays, free gifts and information handouts, then advertising expenditure in 'real' terms[1 2] per head of population will vary between countries, or over time in a given country, as follows:

Other things equal, it will vary:

1. directly with personal income levels[1 3] (real per capita disposable household income);

2. inversely with the overall volume of excess demand (repressed inflation, sellers' markets);

3. inversely with the volume of 'other marketing' (price competition, rebates to distributors, etc.);

4. inversely with the extent of barriers to entry into new markets (i.e., there will be more advertising, the more legal or technical scope there is for enterprises to move into new markets);

5. directly with the extent of barriers to exit from old markets (i.e., there will be more advertising, the more legal or technical restrictions there are on enterprises leaving old, declining markets);

6. directly with the extent of negotiated market exchange as opposed to free supply or administrative allocation in the exchange of goods and services.

It is not possible in practice to quantify the 'volume of other marketing' or the concept of barriers between markets,

---

[1 2] I take this broad definition for convenience, since what Soviet data there are roughly correspond to it. See chapter 3. The difficulties of finding appropriate purchasing power parities for reducing different national advertising expenditure data to a common unit would be very great.

[1 3] Personal income rather than personal consumption or total production, on the grounds that (*a*) personal savings institutions advertise, in the USSR as elsewhere; (*b*) all advertisers compete for shares in total disposable personal income, with the exception of advertisers of producer goods; (*c*) the volume of advertising is more strongly affected by the volume of personal disposable income than by that of GNP or GNP plus intermediate production. (*c*) is an assumption that might not be satisfactory if we were building a quantifiable model to explain international difference in total (not just consumer) advertising volume, but it will do for our present purposes.

and the other main terms are not easy to quantify reliably in international or inter-temporal comparisons. However, these propositions will serve as a basis for organising material and making judgements about it

The socialist economies appear to differ substantially from Western Europe and North America in respect of all these influences on advertising. They clearly differ in private income levels and in the extent of repressed inflation and sellers' markets. The traditional Soviet planning system also includes institutional monopoly arrangements and barriers between markets. This, it is suggested, can operate both to foster and to inhibit advertising.

Finally, and this is not the same thing, the Soviet-type system in some markets has traditionally replaced voluntary purchase entirely by planned allocation. This is true of many exchanges of producer goods, i.e. capital goods and inter-mediate products (materials and semi-finished goods). It is also true of some forms of consumption. The Soviet economy differs from most, perhaps from all, Western economies in the extent to which it meets some demands through public rather than private consumption (e.g. univers-ally imposed free education and large net housing subsidies). These differences all operate to reduce advertising expend-iture, although Soviet citizens do, for example, spend some time and money on advertising to exchange state-owned apartments, rent *dachas*, sell private tuition and so on. It is also true that Soviet planners can and do neglect an unsatisfied market demand in favour of some quite different public good (e.g. the demand for more housing and more cars in favour of defence and space expenditure), but this difference is reflected in personal income levels and in sellers' markets.

Where administrative allocation has been replaced by market relationships, as in Hungary and Yugoslavia, we would expect a weakening of sellers' markets and instit-utional monopolies, with a considerable effect on advertising.

Part I The Soviet Union

2 The Soviet economy and the organisation of Soviet advertising

Introduction

In recent years, and particularly since the early 1960s, there has been a sudden increase in interest in commercial advertising in the USSR. A great many advertising organisations have been created: according to a recent Soviet press report, 'nobody even knows' how many advertising organisations exist in the country; another speaks of forty such organisations in the Ukraine alone.[1] The most developed Soviet advertising, understandably, is in foreign trade, where Soviet suppliers have to operate in Western and some other Comecon markets which are less 'planned' and more competitive than the Soviet home market. But apart from *Vneshtorgreklama*, the foreign trade advertising organisation set up in its present form in 1965 but originating considerably earlier, there is now a whole host of domestic advertising institutions. These include an Inter-departmental Advertising Council linking several ministries, organisations attached to the domestic trade ministries at all-union level and in the Russian and Ukranian republics, advertising departments in the trade administrations of city councils and some advertising sections in production enterprises and other organisations.

Display advertising of consumer goods now appears regularly in the press, most notably in a weekly advertising supplement to the Moscow city evening paper, *Vechernyaya Moskva*. It can also be seen on television, though admittedly in small doses. There has even been a commercially-sponsored television quiz game, and some commercial use of 'editorial'

---

[1] (23); (27).

copy in the press.[2] All the usual media are now used in some degree for commercial advertising, and Soviet books and articles on advertising since the mid-1960s are quite numerous.[3] Rosser Reeves' *Reality in Advertising* and the International Code of Advertising Practice have been translated and published with limited circulation for official use (*'dlya sluzhebnovo pol 'zovaniya'*); a substantial bibliography of international literature on advertising has been published on the same basis.[4]

The extent of this development, and the reasons for it, will be considered in chapters 3 and 4. The purpose of the present chapter is to describe, briefly, the economic environment in which Soviet advertising is conducted and in more detail the origins, functions and administrative subordination of the main advertising organisations themselves.

Some relevant structural differences between the present Soviet economic system and that of the UK (and, broadly, other developed Western countries) should be very briefly outlined. A fuller discussion can be found in a number of books in English.[5]

In general, the Soviet economic system remains a system of highly centralised physical allocation. It has not been fundamentally altered by the post-Khrushchev reforms. It is a mistake to think that the new incentive schemes amount to a Western-style 'profit motive', whatever — precisely — that may be, or even to a clear shift towards market socialism on Yugoslav lines. Most industrial and trade enterprises and some state farms now have a system of management bonuses introduced in the reforms of 1965 onwards. Bonuses are supposed to depend primarily on annual performance as measured (*a*) by the increase in sales of profits and (*b*) by the rate of profit, profits being defined for (*a*) as gross of a

---

[2] (14); (6), p. 114; (18); (36), p. 50. These particular activities are discussed in more detail later on.
[3] See the Bibliography. Hardly anything was published on advertising before the mid-1960s though textbooks on distributive trading usually made a brief reference to it — mainly to shop window display.
[4] (3).
[5] Particularly Alec Nove, *The Soviet Economy* (3rd ed., Allen and Unwin, 1969) and Michael Kaser, *Soviet Economics* (Weidenfeld and Nicholson, 1970).

'capital charge' on fixed and minimum working capital and interest on bank credit, but being defined net of these charges for (*b*). Though these bonuses are deducted from profits, their size is calculated as a percentage of the wage bill, the percentage varying with measured performance according to a variety of coefficients set specially for each enterprise or branch and liable to be changed. This gives a certain bias towards labour-intensive production methods. Obviously this system is not the same as simply relating bonuses to total profits net of interest and depreciation or total sales. Moreover, bonuses are affected by the relation of actual performance to planned performance, and the tendency for enterprise directors to play for low plans in order to make bonuses easier to obtain has apparently not been removed, though it may have been weakened.

At the same time, prices are not generally in the control of the enterprise or even of its superior ministry. Enterprises or combines normally receive an 'assortment plan' from above; this, together with the still fairly centralised control of investment funds, restricts them from moving from one broad field of production into another. The 'proportions' of the economy are therefore subject to central planning and control in some detail. Thus a milk-processing combine may perhaps on its own initiative move into the production of yoghurt but not into the processing of quick-frozen vegetables. Even a production ministry will in this respect have less mobility than a giant corporation like ICI.

Centralised physical allocation of an enterprise's output to users, rather than voluntary sales negotiation between independent parties, is the rule for many producer's goods, and can happen at least on occasion with supplies of consumer goods to the distributive system.[6] Shortages and sellers'

---

[6] According to the First Deputy Minister of Trade for the USSR, S. A. Trifonov, in 1968 his Ministry was responsible for the centralised allocation throughout the country of 404 items, including 67 food items. Supplies between, but not within, the republics were centrally planned for 1200 items. (8), p. 19. Preferential allocation to the major cities, particularly Moscow, still seems to be carried on. Many consumer-goods imported from the West appear to be allocated to these cities only. What allocation by the USSR or republic-level Ministries of Trade can mean to the individual shop or trade organisation is that

markets exist for many products at the retail stage, given the controlled retail prices. The key indicators of performance of an enterprise or combine still tend to be planned by its superior ministry. The incentives to conscientious and energetic planning on the part of administrators at ministry level are widely considered to be inadequate and failures of co-ordination within and between ministries are still frequently criticised.[7] In short, Soviet production and allocation is still in very large measure determined by centralised physical control rather than markets.

Much decision-making in the public sector and in very large private firms in the West may be of a similar kind. The differences are that Western economies have many more autonomous small units, and even the largest firms are themselves operating in markets, including a capital market. The Soviet ministry operates for better or worse in a largely bureaucratic, not a market, environment. Only its labour recruitment and (in some cases) its disposal of output are done via markets.

On the other hand, feedback mechanisms from demand to supply have undoubtedly been strengthened in the last ten years. Incentive payments in production enterprises can and do suffer from failures to adapt assortment, quality and quantity of output to changes in final demand. Trade ordering and sales-related management incentives in internal trade and production do lead to adaptation of the pattern of

---

what it gets need bear little relation to its orders to wholesalers. One shop in Sverdlovsk is described as having ordered for 1968 1700 Rekord televisions and 800 Rassvet televisions and received 788 and 1794 respectively. (25), p. 28. The same sort of thing is described for perfumes in (26), p. 29. The reform does not consistently induce the industrial supplier to meet trade orders, since his bonus depends on a 'sales' total which is unaffected by whether the 'sales' correspond to orders, and his assortment plan specifies major groups of products to be *produced* without reference to whether or not they have been ordered or can be unloaded ('sold') at all. Fines for infringement of sales contracts do not affect bonuses. The article by Yurov is a very clear critique of these arrangements. (38).

[7] Bachurin points out that ministries and their divisions 'have no economic responsibility for the results' of their decisions. (11), p. 11. Academician Trapeznikov proposes a bonus incentive system for ministry staff. (33).

consumer-goods supply to the pattern of demand,[8] though this is weakened by the prevalence of sellers' markets.

It is the net effect of these different organisational influences that determines the volume of marketing expenditure. Overall, the situation in respect of controls, shortages and the general environment of marketing is in some ways reminiscent of early post-war Britain, though the extent of central control is certainly greater.

Soviet advertising organisations
Practically all the Soviet organisations that have the word 'advertising' (*reklama*) in their titles are relatively new. Those that existed in the 1950s began with only a limited range of advertising activity. Typically they supervised the production of equipment for shop-window display — mannequins, etc. — and did little else. On the whole they are creations of the past six years, and their structure and functions are still in an early and rapid state of evolution. There is a prehistory to Soviet advertising, but it is slight and can be quickly sketched.

Advertising organisations developed in Russia before the Revolution, of course. The first advertising office in Moscow is said to have been that of Mettsel, set up in 1878.[9] Mettsel's slogan, 'Advertising is the Engine of Trade', has a well-remembered, if small, niche in Russian commercial history. It is quite often quoted in current Soviet writings on advertising.

The Revolution did not immediately end commercial advertising in Russia. It is true that a Decree on the Introduction of a State Monopoly in Publicity, signed by Lenin and Lunacharsky in 1917, was one of the earliest acts of the new government; its intention was to subject all

---

[8] Particularly through trade ordering at trade fairs. This and other mechanisms, as I have argued in chapter 8 of *The Consumer in the Soviet Economy* (Macmillan, 1968), provide quite substantial feedback. But distributors still complain (they have been doing so for more than ten years) that their orders do not on the whole determine production plans, and deals made at trade fairs are not firm enough, mainly because the industrial suppliers cannot be sure what their own materials supply allocations will be. (8), p. 27; (38).

[9] (5), pp. 11-12.

private advertisements and announcements to censorship and to forbid all paid insertions of advertising material presented as editorial copy. But censorship did not mean abolition. In the New Economic Policy period of 1921-8 when the Soviet Union had a substantial private enterprise sector and much less central control than later on, commercial advertising was still common. It contributed to a positively capitalist extent to the finances of the Soviet press. In 1923 two-thirds of *Izvestiya's* revenue was from advertisements, and they occupied four of its six to eight pages.[10] However, with the industrialisation drive and the creation of the classic Soviet economic system, advertising dwindled to tiny proportions. Press advertising was almost entirely of the film and theatre guide type and there were no specialised intermediary organisations so far as the domestic economy was concerned. Only in the 1960s has advertising begun to revive.

The main advertising organisations now in existence are shown in chart 1 in the appendix to this chapter. They come into four categories: a top-level advertising co-ordinating council; national and republic-level advertising organisations attached to the state and co-operative trade network; advertising departments of local authority trade administrations; and advertising departments in service and industrial ministries, combines and enterprises.

All are in the last resort part of a single administrative unit — the centrally controlled Soviet economy. All Soviet state organisations are formally subordinate to the USSR Council of Ministers and informally to the top leadership, concentrated in the Politburo of the Party Central Committee. They are subject directly or indirectly to centralised planning and control. The co-operative organisations (basically, collective farms and the Central Consumer Co-operative Union which administers rural retail trade) are integrated into the system of plans, allocations and instructions without being formally owned by the state.

[10] Ibid., p. 53. Most of this is said to have been from private firms, but advertising by state organisations was considered quite a reputable activity. Mayakovsky wrote some advertising copy for state enterprises and considered his (untranslateable) slogan for Mossel'prom to be 'poetry of the highest class'.

Vneshtorgreklama, under the Ministry of Foreign Trade, is almost exclusively concerned with, and has a near-monopoly of, foreign trade advertising.[11] It places advertising for foreign clients in Soviet media and prepares and places advertising for Soviet foreign trade organisations. Soviet exporters also make use of foreign agencies, but often via Vneshtorgreklama. It publishes the journal *Soviet Exports* for foreign markets and material about actual or potential imports for the domestic market, notably the bulletin *Inostrannye firmy predlagayut* (*Foreign Firms Offer*). Its staff is of the order of 200, including copy-writers and artists who also work in domestic advertising. It carries out research on advertising methods and effectiveness, and with its foreign links it is, by general consent among Soviet advertising people, the most sophisticated advertising organisation in the Soviet Union. A good deal of the Soviet literature on advertising has been written by Vneshtorgreklama staff, notably D. B. Bekleshov (see Bibliography). Vneshtorgreklama is not formally linked to the domestic advertising organisations discussed below. Its chief importance to Soviet domestic advertising of domestic products is as a technical pace-setter and channel for information on foreign advertising methods.[12]

For domestic advertising there is one organisation that is intended as a supreme co-ordinating body, the Mezhduvedomstvennyi soviet po reklame (Inter-Departmental Council on Advertising, hereafter IDCA). The IDCA currently has the First Deputy Minister of (Internal) Trade for the USSR as chairman, with deputy ministers from the USSR food and light industries, plus the deputy head of Tsentrosoyuz (The Central Union of Consumer Co-operatives) as vice-chairmen, and representatives from the state committees which administer the main media and from the few other national-level organisations, such as Aeroflot, which have a substantial

[11] Soyuztorgreklama has apparently organised some advertising of imports from Hungary and Rumania, but this may well have been channelled through the foreign trade agency.
[12] A UN guide to export marketing in Eastern Europe, by J. R. Mikton, intended primarily for exporters from underdeveloped countries, contains an excellent survey of foreign trade advertising agencies in Comecon countries.

interest in advertising. The council as such is supposed to meet twice yearly, but it has a permanent secretariat provided by the USSR Ministry of Trade, with the principal secretary located in Soyuztorgreklama, the all-union advertising organisation described below. According to one Soviet source, the IDCA has four sections, dealing with the advertising of manufactured goods, the advertising of food products and 'rational nutrition', advertising methodology and aesthetics, and the economics and organisation of advertising, respectively.[13]

The IDCA is a top-level forum in which the chief organisations interested in advertising can get together. It is intended to co-ordinate and plan all Soviet domestic advertising, but it is freely admitted in the Soviet literature and in conversation with Soviet advertising people that this is not yet being done by anyone. The whole subject of central control of advertising will be discussed below. Here it is worth noting only that the IDCA is supposed to do the following things: first, to review all those advertising campaigns that are to be conducted on a national scale, using all the main media, allocate responsibility for them (presumably financial as well as organisational) between ministries and get the ministries concerned to confirm the relevant measures as part of their plans;[14] secondly, to provide some sort of general supervision, methodological guidance and co-ordination (e.g. elimination of duplication) of other advertising plans. In practice, it appears to be not very active. It also appears to be subordinate, via its chairman, to the USSR Trade Ministry. It is sometimes argued that it should be directly subordinate to the Council of Ministers rather than to any one ministry.

Subordinate to the IDCA are three major advertising organisations: Soyuztorgreklama (the All-Union Trade Advertising Combine, hereafter STR), Rostorgreklama (The Russian Republic Trade Advertising Organisation, hereafter RTR), and Ukrtorgreklama (The Ukrainian Republic Trade Advertising Trust, hereafter UTR). These all have dual

[13] (2), p. 107.
[14] (31), p. 55.

subordination, to IDCA and to internal trade ministries: STR to the All-Union (National) Ministry, RTR to the Russian Republic Ministry and UTR to the Ukraine Republic Ministry. These are ministries that administer almost all the urban retail and consumer wholesale trade of the country. Trade in rural areas is run by the consumer co-operative organisation.

These three are the largest domestic advertising organisations in the Soviet Union, and they are the nearest Soviet institutions (apart from Vneshtorgreklama) to Western advertising agencies. They are all rather embryonic and unspecialised organisations, however, by Western standards. Another striking thing about them is that they are attached to internal trade ministries rather than to industry — a significant point which we shall come back to. Their internal organisation varies, but the main subdivisions broadly resemble those of Roskooptorgreklama, shown in chart 2 in the appendix to this chapter.

STR was set up in 1965 and had a head office staff of 95 in April 1970. Like RTR and UTR it consists of more than a head office, however. It combines the intermediary and creative work of an agency with the production of advertising equipment: shop-display equipment, neon signs, printing work and so on. For accounting and control purposes it is an independent unit and is expected to cover its costs from revenue and to earn some profit. In 1969 it was responsible for the administration of eleven plants. It also had nineteen regional branches in different parts of the country.[15] Some at least of its regional branches themselves combine agency and production work. Indeed, the STR Moldavian Republic Kombinat, for example, is said to be developing a wide range of agency services, including market research.[16]

STR has a general supervising and co-ordinating role in relation to all the advertising work of the state distributive system in all the lesser republics, i.e. all except the Russian Republic and the Ukraine.

This clearly covers its own branch network, whose units are subordinate also to their republic-level trade ministries. In

[15] (23). The author was Deputy General Director of STR.
[16] (12), p. 50.

practice it does not seem to control or co-ordinate the work of advertising departments of local (city and regional, i.e. below republic level) authority trade administrations (see below). Its annual plan and its turnover figures overlap with those of RTR in that both include Russian Republic expenditures in some national advertising campaigns, but it does not have powers to control either RTR or UTR activities. Any overall national control has to be at the level of the IDCA.

STR is an All-Union combine — a fairly lofty status — and though attached to the USSR Ministry of Trade has a separate head office building several metro stops away from the Ministry. RTR, on the other hand, is located in the Russian Republic Trade Ministry building and works closely with other divisions of that ministry. Its head is subordinate to a Deputy Minister.

RTR was founded in 1958. It was originally the ministry division responsible for the production of retail display equipment and has expanded into agency work.[17] Although it is inside the Ministry, it prepares its own plan, which apparently is not usually changed from above. In April 1970 RTR controlled seven *kombinaty* in seven cities of the Russian Republic. Its work includes a great deal, but by no means all, of the trade advertising of the Republic. Local trade administration advertising is planned separately, and much of Moscow trade advertising in particular, is outside RTR's control. Since the Russian Republic population in early 1970 was about 130 million out of a national total of somewhat over 240 million, RTR still has a large empire.

UTR, its Ukrainian counterpart, was set up in 1960 and has a similar background. Its status, however, is that of a trust (the Ukraine is the great breeding-ground for trusts, combines and other multi-plant concerns which are distinct from — though subordinate to — ministries and ministry divisions) and its Kiev head office has a building of its own. In May 1970 it controlled eleven *kombinaty* and had a total labour force, including production workers, of 2500. Its director hopes to have UTR branches in all the *oblast* (regional) centres of the Ukraine by 1975.

---

[17] (2), p. 107; (29), p. 53.

The state trading organisations of other republics have a variety of advertising *kombinaty*, subject to STR. These range from small workshops producing mannequins for shop windows to embryonic agencies, with the Baltic states, as usual, reputedly in the lead.

There are parallel organisations, generally smaller, in the rural domestic trade system of the consumer co-operatives. Glavkooptorgreklama is the national-level organisation, with Roskooptorgreklama (chart 2) in the Russian Republic and Ukrkooptogreklama in the Ukraine. These, too, have regional *kombinaty*.[18] Chart 3 is an organisation chart for a consumer co-operative regional *kombinat*. It is almost certainly more of a prescription for the future than a description of the present — two genres that are always hard to disentangle in Soviet economic literature — and perhaps describes the most developed of the existing *kombinaty* in, for example, the STR system (see above).

In addition, there are advertising departments (AD in chart 1) in some city and regional trade administrations. There are also some in the biggest department stores. The work of these departments is quite extensive; they place some advertising with local television, radio and press as well as producing retail display equipment. There seems to be little information at the centre about the scale and composition of their work, and, *a fortiori*, little central control over it. However, co-ordination at local level by, e.g., a city Inter-Departmental Council on Advertising has occurred and is encouraged by higher organs.[19]

Finally, there are advertising organisations in some industrial ministries, e.g., the Soyuzprodooformlenie trust of the USSR Ministry of the Food Industry and Rospishchetorgreklama in its subordinate Russian Republic Ministry. There are also advertising departments in some large All-Union organisations, notably in Aeroflot and in some industrial combines and enterprises.[20] Another type of organisation which is increasingly active in advertising is the group of ministries and local organisations running services such as

---

[18] (6), pp. 8, 10, 13, 14, 21.
[19] The work of the Gorky council is discussed as a model for this sort of local co-ordination in (9b), pp. 3-10.
[20] (1), p. 14.

laundering and dry cleaning. On the whole, however, advertising organisations have not been created by producers on anything approaching the scale of the trade advertising organisations. While some producer ministries have developed market research organisations, the nuclei of advertising agencies seem to be developing entirely within the distributive system.

What seems to be the recommended structure for advertising departments in industry is briefly as follows: first, advertising sections in All-Union and/or republic ministries, co-ordinating the work of advertising departments in subordinate enterprises; second, enterprise advertising departments or groups under the deputy director for 'disposals' (sales, but *à la Russe*) plus, interestingly, a separate export advertising department under the deputy director for exports if the enterprise is an export producer; the advertising department under the deputy director for sales is to work particularly with the planning department (under the deputy director/ chief economist) and the design department (under the deputy director/chief engineer). The model advertising department is supposed to consist of art, editorial and exhibition sections, with scope for creative work is some cases as well as the commissioning of agencies.[21] It is safe to say that few, if any, such departments yet exist in Soviet industry. On the other hand some industrial enterprises have taken the initiative in commissioning advertising, though they would normally have to get approval from their main administration (within their ministry) for the allocation of funds to advertising.

These, then, are the main types of advertising organisation. None of them could quite be described as an advertising agency. It is widely agreed among Soviet advertising people, however, that some of them should evolve into institutions with the functions, broadly, of Western agencies. The commonest opinion is that such agencies will come into being when there are enough advertising specialists with enough experience to staff a number of separate concerns whose work consists only of the specialist activities characteristic of

[21] (1), pp. 12-19.

a Western agency, and that the present shortage of advertising specialists is the chief problem.

There is however another view which is more cautious. It stresses that the exact functions of advertising in the Soviet economy are not yet clear, and that the future shape of advertising organisations cannot be fixed until everybody has a much clearer idea of what Soviet advertising is supposed to do.

There certainly is no clear agreement on what the precise functions of Soviet advertising will be. What can be described as the official line is not too helpful. It is largely an assertion that socialist advertising will avoid various evils ascribed to capitalist advertising, being superior in aim and (therefore) in method.

The nearest thing to a summary of Soviet official policy in advertising seems to be contained in the recommendations of the 1957 Prague Conference of Advertising Workers of Socialist Countries. In a book published twelve years later, in 1969, these aims are still endorsed.[22] Elsewhere in the literature they continue to be alluded to, and in interviews with people in Soviet advertising their general drift was repeated to me by almost everyone I spoke to.

The aims listed by the Prague Conference were as follows (I have translated literally, to capture the flavour):

first, to educate people's tastes, develop their requirements (*potrebnosti*) and, thus, actively form demand (*spros*) for goods;

second, to help the consumer by giving him information about the most rational means (forms) of consumption;

thirdly, to help to raise the culture of trade (i.e. to improve service to the consumer in retail trade).

From these aims it follows, according to Degtyarev and Kornilov,[23] that socialist advertising must have the following characteristics:

first, ideological content (*ideinost*). It must conform with party and state policy in the area of the raising of material and cultural levels of development, and also in observing the

[22] (5), p. 15.
[23] (5), pp. 16-17.

principles of socialist realism in creative work in advertising. It must orient consumers towards the improvement of living conditions, rational consumption and rational use of leisure;

second, truthfulness (about the goods advertised);

third, concreteness. Good arguments and data must be used. In design, this rules out unjustified formalism and methods unintelligible to a wide audience;

fourth, practicality. It must start from the product and the state of the market and aim at the consumer. It must not waste resources (in the sense that advertising expenditure must show a good return);

fifth, planned character. It must be linked to production and trade plans.

These propositions do not mean a great deal. However, it would be a mistake to dismiss them as entirely meaningless, and irrelevant to the practical operations of Soviet advertising organisations (their relation to the content of Soviet advertising is discussed in chapter 4 below).

There is an important emphasis on developing new requirements. The Russian word *potrebnosti* (requirements) is quite distinct from that for effective demand (*spros*) in the demand and supply relationship expressed on markets. Its sense is more that of aspirations or standards, and it is invariably used in an approving sense. It is felt to be good that people should acquire new expectations about their consumption of goods and services.

Connected with this is another emphasis familiar in the Soviet Union: on teaching, informing, educating people. Such things as rational norms of consumption are not merely conceivable, they are already known. They can be formulated by experts and inculcated by advertising. Party policy, expressed in plans, is therefore rational as well as ideologically based, and demand can be moulded towards planned supply by informative, not deceptive or emotive, advertising.

The function implied for advertising organisations is the marketing of planned output. In practice, Soviet advertising people mostly describe their work at present as the advertising of 'new and sufficient [*dostatochnye*] goods'. The shifting of stocks of consumer goods (predominantly held by retailers) which are above the centrally determined distributive stock norms (stock: turnover ratios) is sometimes given as a basic purpose of advertising.[24] Simultaneously diverting demand from 'scarce' items, it helps to reduce macro-economic disequilibrium in consumer markets with predominantly fixed prices. New goods are included only to the extent that they are also 'sufficient'.

In the current prevailing view, therefore, specialised advertising organisations need not concern themselves very much with market research. They are mainly linked with the distribution system. The product-group wholesale divisions of the All-Union or republic ministries of trade provide them with information on products to be advertised, on the basis of stock and sales data. Other forms of market research are used mainly for production planning. In general, the advertising organisations are supposed to have little to do with product design and the production end of marketing as a whole.

This is the basis of present organisation. It is quite likely to be changed, as the following sections show. When these specialised organisations act as intermediaries between advertisers and media, as they quite often do, the basis on which they are paid is not clear. It appears to be by fees rather than commission, but there is probably no standard practice. Broader organisational questions — who decides to spend money on advertising, how it is financed and how advertising campaigns are planned — will be discussed in chapter 4 below.

[24] (2), p. 79.

APPENDIX TO CHAPTER 2

Organisation charts

CHART 1   Location of advertising organisations in the formal administrative structure of the Soviet economy

1. National level: (A) USSR ministries of

2. Republic level: republic ministries of trade of

3. Local (oblast, etc., city) level:

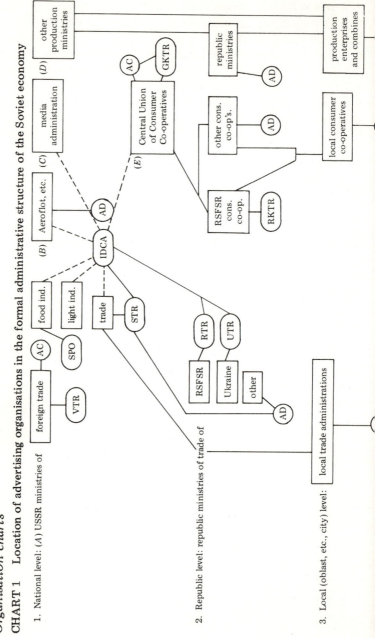

Key: All advertising organisations are denoted by circles enclosing their names. IDCA = Inter-Departmental Council on Advertising; VTR = Vneshtorgreklama; STR = Soyuztorgreklama; RTA = Rostorgreklama; UTR = Ukrtorgreklama; GTR = Glavkooptorgreklama; RKTR = Roskooptorgreklama; SPO = Soyuzprodooformlenie; AC = Advertising Council. AD = One or more departments of advertising. Solid lines denote subordination of lower to higher bodies. Where they are horizontal the relationship is consultative. Broken lines denote representation in the IDCA.

Notes: 'National-level' bodies are generally subordinate to the USSR Council of Ministers, with much of their work planned by the State Planning Commission (USSR Gosplan), which is itself a state committee. The USSR Council of Ministers is in turn informally subject to the top leadership, i.e., the Politburo of the Central Committee of the Communist Party of the Soviet Union.

At other levels most organisations have a dual subordination, to a Republic Council of Ministers or a local Soviet and also to the corresponding body at the level above their own — e.g. Republic Ministries of Trade to the USSR Ministry of Trade as well as to their Republic Council of Ministers, and local Trade Administrations to their Republic Ministry of Trade as well as to their city council.

Production enterprises and combines may be directly subordinate to a national-level (All-Union) ministry or subordinate to a republic-level ministry which is in turn subordinate to a national-level (Union-Republic) ministry.

33

CHART 2   Internal structure of a republic-level advertising organisation (Roskooptorgreklama)

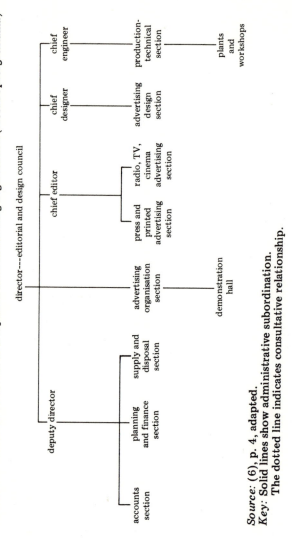

director---editorial and design council

deputy director

accounts section

planning and finance section

supply and disposal section

advertising organisation section

demonstration hall

chief editor

press and printed advertising section

radio, TV, cinema advertising section

chief designer

advertising design section

chief engineer

production-technical section

plants and workshops

Source: (6), p. 4, adapted.
Key: Solid lines show administrative subordination.
 The dotted line indicates consultative relationship.

34

CHART 3   An advertising-production unit (kombinat)

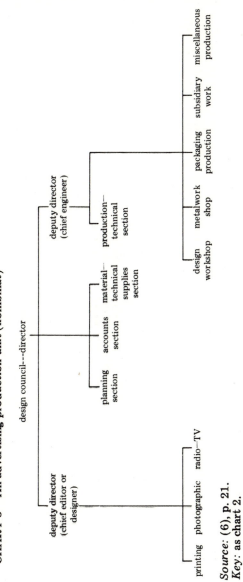

design council--director

deputy director (chief editor or designer)

- printing
- photographic
- radio--TV

deputy director (chief engineer)

- planning section
- accounts section
- material-technical supplies section
- production-technical section
  - design workshop
  - metalwork shop
  - packaging production
  - subsidiary work
  - miscellaneous production

Source: (6), p. 21.
Key: as chart 2.

35

3 Soviet advertising expenditure

Volume

There are no good, comprehensive data on the volume of Soviet advertising, published or unpublished. The IDCA, responsible for national co-ordination of advertising, appears to have data only for the major advertising organisations, STR, RTR and UTR, plus information on the overall size of funds earmarked for advertising throughout the distributive system (i.e. the retail and wholesale networks controlled by the USSR Ministry of Trade and Central Union of Consumer Co-operatives). The former data, for the 1970 annual plan, were quoted to me in interviews. There are references to the latter in the literature, for 1966 and 1967.[1] To what extent the two kinds of data overlap is not clear. A great deal of the advertising financed by the distributive system, but by no means all, is channelled through STR, RTR and UTR (see chapter 2 above). At the same time, some of these organisations' turnover is financed by manufacturing and service organisations. Moreover, actual advertising expenditure by the distributive system corresponds roughly, but not exactly, to the official advertising appropriation (see next section).

Consequently only a rough judgement on the order of magnitude is possible. The published figures for 'trade advertising' in 1966 and 1967 are 27.7 and 53.0 million rubles. These figures appear to be derived from the financial reporting of trade organisations. The latter consists of expenditure by local trade organisations of 34.6 million rubles and by Republic Ministries of Trade of 18.4 million

[1] (8), p. 143 and (31), p. 57, respectively. The small scale of total Soviet advertising can be indicated by the following data for 1968, for 35 provinces (*oblasti*) covering perhaps a third of the population: a total of 200 advertisements, 100 radio and over 1000 press and 'over 16,000 screen days' with cinema advertising. (29), p. 54.

rubles. The coverage of the 1966 figure in respect of advertisers is not explained. It might refer only to the expenditures of local organisations. The 1967 figure is equal to 0.042 per cent of retail turnover.[2] This roughly tallies with the advertising appropriation rate in the distributive system, which is said to be around 0.03 − 0.04 per cent of turnover. Given this correspondence, we can reasonably conclude that the 1967 figure is the official return of advertising expenditure by the distributive system.

The volume of advertising by exporters to the USSR and the volume financed by Soviet producers, as opposed to distributors, should be added to this total but are not available. However, it appears that 55 per cent and 30 per cent of foreign advertising expenditure in some recent year were on technical and other journals and newspapers respectively. The remaining 15 per cent would be predominantly on trade fairs and exhibitions.[3] The space taken by foreign advertisers in the Soviet press appears to be not more than that taken by domestic advertisers, and Soviet domestic press advertising is a relatively small part of the Soviet total (see chapter 4). Even allowing for differences in the publications used by foreign and domestic advertisers and possible differences in the rates charged to them in the same publications, total advertising expenditure in the USSR by foreign concerns must be relatively small. The volume of advertising financed by Soviet manufacturing and service concerns must also be relatively small (chapter 4). A maximum plausible guess at the 1967 total would therefore be about 100 million rubles or about 0.08 per cent of retail turnover. A best estimate would be more like 75 million rubles, or about 0.06 per cent of retail turnover.

Before one can attach any meaning to these figures, let alone compare them with Western data, it is necessary to know their coverage and their validity as a measure of resources allocated to advertising. Coverage can be judged from the detailed 1970 plan figures for the major advertising

[2] Retail turnover from (39), p. 609. This includes sales of catering enterprises and the relatively small sales on the urban peasant markets, on which neither sales volume nor prices are directly controlled.
[3] (1), p. 54.

organisations (see chapter 4). It includes media advertising covered by the most recent Advertising Association data for the UK; press, television, radio, poster and other outdoor and cinema.[4] It also includes some window and shop display, some packaging, a substantial volume of catalogues, circulars, etc., and some expenditure on trade affairs. These categories correspond to some concepts of 'below-the-line' advertising expenditure,[5] and would be in category B of the International Advertising Association classification of advertising expenditure data. They were included in earlier Advertising Association and other estimates of UK advertising expenditure,[6] but the national data on them usually have rather uncertain coverage. Finally, the Soviet figures exclude small advertisements by private individuals, i.e. the equivalent of part of Western classified advertising.

The problem of what these money totals mean is more difficult. In general, Soviet prices are relatively poor measures of the scarcity of products and resources. In the present context, for example, space rates in the press usually seem both low and arbitrary to Western exporters. Data on domestic rates support this impression (see the appendix to this chapter). Admittedly this is only in relation to circulation, since other information on the value of the space to advertisers is lacking. In the sense, however, that there is evidence of a shortage of press advertising space, i.e. excess demand at existing rates (see the next section), rates probably are too low. The same may be true of other media. It also appears that some services to advertisers are supplied free of charge. As with many other value totals in the Soviet economy, advertising expenditure figures are probably a worse measure of the opportunity cost of the inputs used in terms of other possible uses forgone than apparently equivalent figures from market economies.

[4] *Advertising Expenditure 1964—1968*, supplement to *The Advertising Quarterly* (Summer 1969).
[5] See Ken Wilmshurst, 'Above or Below? Where to Draw the Line', *Advertising Quarterly* (Spring 1970), pp. 13—19.
[6] For the earlier UK series, see Ralph Harris and Arthur Seldon, *Advertising and the Public* (André Deutsch, 1962) p. 44. A recent estimate for UK promotional selling costs is £300—400m. p.a. (*The Times*, 14 May 1970, p. 25), or 60—80 per cent of the Advertising Association estimate of UK media advertising expenditure in 1968.

Still, Soviet wholesale and other producer prices are mostly cost-plus, costing is not totally dissimilar to Western practices, and the valuation problem should be small enough to ignore. It is obvious to anyone visiting Russia that advertising is still only on a very small scale by Western European or North American standards. The few and sketchy figures available for the USSR are enough to give a rough indication of the extent of this disparity.

One way of doing this is to try to duplicate for the USSR a conventional measure of the relative importance of advertising in the national economy which is frequently used for Western economies: advertising expenditure as a percentage of household consumption expenditure.[7]

There are no Soviet published data on total household expenditure but it can be derived with reasonable confidence from a combination of Soviet sources.[8] The result, private consumption expenditure at market prices of about 140 milliard rubles in 1967, gives a maximum plausible percentage figure for advertising expenditure in relation to household consumption of 0.07. The true figure is more likely to be around 0.05.

The most recent data on advertising expenditure for the UK are, as we have seen, of narrower coverage. From earlier

[7] See Economists Advisory Group, *The Economics of Advertising* (Advertising Association, 1967) pp. 9—16, for the shortcomings of this measure, and possible alternatives. In the Introduction (n.13) it is argued that there is a causal relationship between household income, rather than expenditure, and advertising expenditure, but we are not interested in causal relationships here.

[8] 1967 'personal consumption' in the Soviet statistical handbook for 1968 ((39), p. 571) or 144.0 milliard ('000 million) rubles excludes most expenditure on services. It also includes an allowance for the depreciation of the housing stock (which probably exceeds personal household expenditure on housing) and, according to (7), p. 117, consumption in 'social institutions individually serving the population' (e.g. food in hospitals, and possibly a great deal more). Western estimates of Soviet household expenditure are usually derived from Soviet published data on wages, other earned income, transfer payments, personal taxation and savings. Data on money income in agriculture and the valuation of the (substantial) volume of income in kind in agriculture are the main problems. On this basis Western-definition household expenditure in 1967 was about 140 milliard rubles. (Ratios of other income to pre-tax wages and salaries from (4), pp. 23, 36, 85. Wages and salaries total from (39), pp. 551, 555, 556. Personal taxation and recorded net increase in household savings from (39), pp. 774, 597).

data on advertising expenditure on a wider and roughly comparable definition (see above), the comparable UK percentage in 1961 was 2.6. Combining more recent Advertising Association estimates for advertising expenditure in a narrower sense with an estimate of £300—400 m. p.a. for other promotional selling costs,[9] one gets figures of 2.9 to 3.3 per cent for the UK in 1968.

Obviously the difference is enormous. It would be slightly reduced if advertising expenditure in each country were expressed as a percentage of household consumption at factor cost. i.e. net indirect taxes and subsidies on items of household consumption. But the effect would only be slight.[10] This very large difference seems compatible with casual observation and with occasional physical data on advertising, e.g. that the total annual number of Soviet press advertisements has recently been 12,000—15,000.[11]

The difference is so large that, despite all the doubts surrounding this crude comparison, it seems to rule out the possibility that the low level of Soviet advertising expenditure could be fully or even largely explained by the relatively low level of per capita real personal income. Soviet per capita personal income levels in the mid-1960s were of the order of a half of UK levels.[12] For the UK, estimates of advertising expenditure going back to 1938 show it to have been in much the same ratio to GNP and consumption expenditure then as in 1958—61.[13] One could make a fair case for UK

[9] Harris and Seldon, *Advertising and the Public*, p. 44; The Times (14 May 1970).
[10] Elsewhere I have estimated total indirect taxation net of subsidies in the mid-1960s to be equal to about 30 per cent of Soviet household consumption expenditure, compared with about 15 per cent in the UK. (Hanson, *The Consumer in the Soviet Economy* (Macmillan, 1968) chapter 6). But since 1965 the revenue from Soviet turnover tax, the main indirect tax, which falls preponderantly on consumer goods, has risen more slowly than household expenditure and almost certainly less than subsidies to items of consumption, notably housing and meat. The two countries' net indirect tax/consumption expenditure ratios have therefore been converging.
[11] (1), p. 60. How classified-type advertisements were counted is not explained.
[12] Hanson, *The Consumer* chapter 4.
[13] Harris and Seldon, *Advertising and the Public* p. 44. For the Advertising Association series referred to above, expressed as a percentage of GNP at market prices, the figures are: 1938, 1.7%; 1948, 1.0%; 1956, 1.6%; 1958, 1.7%; 1960, 1.9%; 1961, 1.8%.

1938 personal consumption or real income levels being on average equal to or less than Soviet levels in 1967. Or, at least, one could do so in so far as such different bundles of things can be compared at all across such gaps of time and space. If this is so, advertising expenditure in the Soviet Union must be relatively very low.

The main elements in the explanation of the low level of Soviet advertising expenditure (see the Introduction) therefore seem to be: first, the extent of sellers' markets (shortages and price controls); second, the extent of institutional monopolies in the Soviet economy, which weaken competitive pressures to incur advertising expenditure; and third, the extent of administrative allocation, as opposed to negotiated sale between independent parties. This last applies in some degree to the exchange of consumer goods between producers and distributors and in very substantial degree to the exchange of producer goods between producers; the former presumably reduces pressures on producers, as opposed to distributors, to advertise and the latter reduces industrial advertising.

On the other hand, Soviet advertising expenditure is growing. This growth is considered in the next section.

Growth and constraints on the supply of advertising
Soviet advertising expenditure appears to be growing fairly fast, but not exceptionally so. The 1966 and 1967 figures for trade advertising quoted in the previous section may be comparable, but on the cautious view that the figure of 27.7 million rubles for 1966 is comparable only to the 'trade enterprises and organisations' figure of 34.6 million rubles for 1967, there was an increase in this major category of about 25 per cent between those years. Staff in the major advertising organisations spoke in April-May 1970 of current annual rates of increase in their turnover of about 20 per cent.

The true growth rate for advertising expenditure as a whole in the 1960s could be well above or well below these figures of 20—25 per cent. Some advertising activities have certainly expanded faster, and others may have risen more slowly — which would hardly be surprising. For example, the total number of advertising films made for the cinema in the USSR is said to have been sixty-two in 1965 and only three in 1960,[14] an average annual growth of 83.3 per cent. Planned expenditure on television advertising in the Ukraine for 1970 was said to be fifteen times greater than actual 1965 expenditure. On the other hand, the annual advertising revenue of the *Izvestiya* Sunday supplement, *Nedelya* (*The Week*), was reported to have risen from 9244 rubles in 1960 to 32,901 rubles in 1967,[15] a more modest growth rate of 19.9 per cent per annum. Obviously this information does not amount to much, but the overall impression is not one of explosive growth. After all, initial levels around 1960 were exceptionally low in all media. And there is the evidence of early post-war growth rates of advertising expenditure in Western countries in a period of recovery and decontrol. One might guess that if the Soviet economy were being similarly decontrolled, growth rates of 40 per cent or more (part of which would be rising media rates) would be very likely.

If, as seems likely, Soviet advertising expenditure was rising more slowly than this in the 1960s, part of the explanation is simply that the Soviet economy has not been substantially de-controlled. But it seems also that, at least from about 1965 onwards, demand for advertising services had tended to outrun supply. The level of advertising expenditure in any one year has almost certainly been held down by constraints on the supply side. The rate of growth may also have been held down, though this is less clear.

The main constraints are the result either of past history, reflected in the shortages of specialised equipment and skills needed in advertising, or of the continuation of the system of central control in the advertising media themselves. The latter is only a particular example of the general effect of traditional Soviet controls on the volume of advertising. It is worth singling out because central control over the media affects the supply of advertising services while central control over suppliers of other goods and services (along with the influence of income levels) affects the demand side. Producers and distributors generally might come to have every possible incentive to advertise; the quantity of advertising can

[14] (2), p. 120.
[15] (5), p. 54.

still be held down to some extent by a lack of incentives or means on the part of the media to supply space and time for advertising. There is, finally, a special financial constraint on the demand side when organisations wishing to advertise run up against a low limit on their advertising appropriation set by a higher organ.

Specifically, the main obstacles on the supply side to growth that are mentioned are the following. First shortages of centrally allocated materials. According to Nastenko, deputy director of STR,[16] his organisation is — or was in 1969 — classified among the low-priority 'other organisations' by Gosplan and Gossnab (the State Committee which plans and controls materials allocations). According to him, available supplies of advertising materials and equipment were only 10 to 40 per cent of applications. STR received — probably for 1969 — only 5 per cent of its application for printing paper (and only four out of the fifty mobile towers for installing neon signs that it put in for — capital equipment supplies are discussed below). He said the planners were increasing supplies by about 10 per cent a year without realising that this meant a growing shortfall. In general, applications for material supplies to advertising were being met only to the extent of about one-third. 'In the past six months' (? first half of 1969) demand for advertising had risen two- to three-fold while the capacity of advertising organisations had risen by 5 to 10 per cent. Supplies to advertising organisations should be included in the national plan and the national direction of advertising should be centred in one organisation (presumably STR). The arithmetic is impressionist and the author is an interested party, but his general view of the situation seems to be correct.

Shortages of newsprint are frequently said to limit the amount of press advertising. Early in 1968, before it introduced a weekly advertising supplement, *Vechernyaya Moskva* was the only Soviet paper devoting one whole page out of its four, on five days of the week, to advertising, and had a two- to three months waiting-list for advertisements.[17]

---

[16] (23).
[17] (37), p. 43.

Nedelya, it is said, could more than treble its receipts from advertising if it could allocate a whole page to it.[18] A chief editor in one advertising organisation, however, told me that more newsprint would be allocated for advertising if the excess demand for it were larger, and it is not clear that it is in total very large now.

The second obstacle is shortages of fixed capital equipment. This is said to be perpetuated by the planners in some cases as well as inherited from the past. STR apparently had a half-million ruble order from the 'Krasnaya zarya' knitwear enterprise for prospectuses, catalogues and packaging which it was quite unable to meet for lack of specialised printing equipment. There were said to be no plans even to produce the equipment needed.[19] The lack of appropriate printing equipment limits the quality of posters, many of which are still hand-painted.[20] Shortages of studio space and equipment are said to limit the output of commercials for television and cinemas though, in the case of television, at least, faults in recent planning were not blamed and the big new studio at Ostankino was expected to fill the gap.[21]

The third obstacle is the system of controls and incentives in the media. The clearest examples available concern the press, but they are representative of a general problem in the media.

Press advertising is still relatively small in quantity (cf. the total of 12,000 − 15,000 advertisements annually in the press, cited in the previous section). Many Soviet periodicals are cheaply produced, have large circulations (see the appendix to this chapter) and are apparently profitable. It is said that the national and big-city dailies, with only four or six pages, do not need to carry any advertising to make a profit. In any case, as long as state subsidies are given to periodicals that do not make a profit no Soviet periodical needs advertising to survive. Only a central policy decision would force it to take advertising.

On the other hand, if its management has an incentive to

[18] (2), p. 54.
[19] (27).
[20] (5), p. 63.
[21] (2), pp. 118, 120, 162.

raise non-subsidy revenue, whether or not there is a subsidy, one would expect it to be interested in carrying advertising. The post-1965 reform system extends, in principle, to newspapers. Their staff should, therefore, earn bonuses on profit and revenue performance. They should be interested, within limits set by the special conditions of the new bonus scheme, in raising profits and therefore in carrying advertising.

There are, however, at least three things that restrict this interest. In the first place, restricted supplies of newsprint combine with requirements on the part of higher organs about the editorial items that must be included to limit the space that can be allocated on the editor's own initiative to advertising. This is the industrial enterprise's supply allocations and assortment plan translated into the field of newspaper publishing.

Secondly, there is the well-known problem of 'hidden reserves': the tendency of managers of production units to try to operate below capacity in order to avoid being set more ambitious targets. One would expect this to occur in the Soviet press as well as in Soviet industry.

Thirdly there is the problem, familiar from industry, that higher organs often do not in fact let 'their' enterprises do all the things they are supposed to be able to do in the new system. The newspaper staff may not in fact be allowed their bonuses from profit, and the editor may not be allowed to take on extra staff needed to handle advertising even though they would more than earn their keep, although he should under the new system have some powers to 'manoeuvre' his staff as long as he stays beneath his monthly wage fund ceilings.

These difficulties were described by the editor of the provincial daily in Nizhnyi Tagil, the *Tagil'skii rabochii*,[22] in 1968. His paper had at that time a circulation of 80,000 and an annual gross revenue of over half a million rubles, of which 100,000 came from advertising. It carried thirty to forty advertisements per issue. In the past it had made a loss at a much lower circulation (25,000) but was now profitable

[22] (37), p. 42.

and paid 200,000 rubles a year to the regional press administration, its immediate superior body.

The newspaper had developed advertising initially because the staff were allowed to keep some of the above-plan profit from it as quarterly bonuses. This had been stopped from above, despite the introduction of the new reform system which was intended to encourage precisely this sort of arrangement. The paper was also unable to get permission to take on more staff to handle advertising. It therefore stopped taking any more, having no interest in doing so, and actually losing by it from the increased and unrewarded work-load on the existing staff. When the regional press administration asked, as a favour, for an above-plan profit payment from the paper of 20,000 rubles to help it out of financial trouble, the editor offered 30,000 which he could get from increased advertising provided he could get a 2—3 per cent allowance on costs for extra bonuses in return. He was told the financial controllers would not allow this, and the deal fell through.

It is very likely that this sort of continued close central control over the media often produces similar results, limiting the supply of media space and time for advertising.

The final constraint on the growth of advertising expenditure that operates to keep the total below what production and distribution enterprises wish to incur is the financial control on advertising appropriations at enterprise level. The very small appropriation of 0.03 to 0.04 per cent of turnover to advertising by trade organisations has been mentioned above. Advertisers are limited by this, and it is quite often suggested that it should be raised. The decision to raise it would probably have to be made at USSR Gosplan level, and almost certainly not below USSR ministry of trade level.

The difficulty is part of a more general one. Retail and wholesale gross margins are centrally determined and extremely low. In 1968, retail gross margins for the whole state and co-operative system excluding catering were 8.79 per cent of turnover. The retail net margin was 1.83 per cent.[23] Wage increases and improvements in retail services have raised retail costs (gross less net margins) from 5.74 to 6.96 per cent

[23] (39), pp. 636, 638.

of turnover between 1960 and 1968. The natural reluctance of policy-makers to raise the cost of living has ruled out substantial retail price increases in recent years, and retail net margins are under great pressure. Wage increases in 1965 and 1968 necessitated once-for-all subsidies to the distributive system. The levels of gross margins of specific items are centrally set and are believed by people in distribution to lead in many cases to net losses on the handling of particular items. The power to negotiate trade discounts between trade and industrial organisations within certain limits has been asked for as a remedy,[24] but the overall problem is still severe.

The result is that allocations of expenditure to advertising above the fixed appropriations can be made only at ministry level, for which time and information are often inadequate. Industrial enterprises are often better able to allocate funds from profits to advertising, since they are often much more profitable than trade organisations under the present structure of centrally fixed prices and margins. But they tend to lack the incentive to do so.

[24] (8), pp. 22—3.

APPENDIX TO CHAPTER 3

TABLE A3.1   Space rates to domestic advertisers in the Soviet press, 1970

	circulation ('000)	rate per page ('000 rubles)
newspapers		
Vechernyaya Moskva		
(Evening Moscow)	300	6
Weekly advertising supplement to *VM*	—	1.4
Moskovskaya Pravda		
(Moscow Pravda)	300	5
Leninskoe Znamya	300	5
Sovetskaya Torgovlya		
(3x weekly for trade workers)	1000	5
Trud	4500	6
Gudok		
(railway workers' paper)	1000	6
Ekonomicheskaya Gazeta		
(economic and management weekly)	600	1.6
Meditsinskaya Gazeta		
(for medical workers)	500	6
Sovetskaya Rossiya		
(weekly)	—	6
journals		
Zdorov'e (Health)	11,200	1.8
Rabotnitsa		
(Women Worker)	11,027	1.8
Novye Tovary		
(New Goods)	411	0.3

Note: These are approximate print order figures. It would be odd if more were printed than are normally sold. On the other hand a substantial proportion of sales in some cases, particularly of the more specialised periodicals, is by institutional subscription, e.g. to workplaces, libraries, etc. It is conceivable that in some cases many copies taken on subscription are not read. I have no evidence of this, but some of the differences in rates are hard to explain otherwise.
Source: interviews.

4 The Nature and Functions of Soviet Advertising

Product-mix

There are no systematic data avaible on the distribution of advertising between product groups in the Soviet Union, even for the major advertising organisations. But the main features are fairly clear.

The advertising organisations see their work as concentrated on 'new and sufficient' goods, as was pointed out in chapter 2. 'Sufficient' means not in short supply (*defitsitnyi*). *Defitsitnyi* is a conventional term, thoroughly familiar to the population at large, denoting products for which demand exceeds supply at state retail prices. These two concepts are appropriate to an economic system in which quantities, not prices, are adjusted to attain equilibrium in individual markets. It is true that this happens in many markets in a Western economy. However, there is much more frequent price adjustment in market economies, even in markets with administered oligopoly prices. Inflationary pressure is common to both systems, so that the consumer tends in the West to be faced with rising prices and in a Soviet-type economy with shortages.

Precisely how the two categories of sufficient and *defitsitnyi* goods are distinguished in Soviet practice is not clear. For practical purposes, it seems, a 'sufficient' consumer good is one for which distributive stocks exceed stock norms, and a *defitsitnyi* product is one to which the opposite applies. This criterion is less than perfect because stock norms are only rough rules of thumb. In the past they have been adjusted on purely financial grounds.[1]

In the Soviet advertising context new goods are in fact a special case of sufficient goods. There are some new goods for which a strong demand exists without advertising before they have even appeared on the market. For them consumer display advertising is not needed. An example is the new Soviet 'Fiat' from the Togliatti plant.

Some products not marketed so far to the general public by state organisations are familiar to many Russians via Western visitors and information from the West, for example jeans, pop records, Western cigarettes and (until recently) stainless steel razor blades. A substantial market for them already exists. Thus the demonstration effect of the West performs some of the functions that Soviet marketing would have if the West did not exist or if the USSR was technologically and quantitatively ahead of the West in consumer goods generally.[2] Soviet consumer display advertising of new goods, in conditions of repressed inflation and a large Western demonstration effect, is concentrated on unfamiliar new goods for which demand is small. There is a large class of familiar new goods that do not (given planned supply levels and prices) need it.

The products on which advertising has been concentrated, then, are of two main kinds: goods (or services) that are both new and 'sufficient', and goods that are 'sufficient' but not new.

[1] Because the distributive organisations had to cover only above-norm stocks with bank credit, on which they had to pay interest, while stock-holding up to the norm was covered by interest-free grants. Raising the norms therefore reduces the distributive system's indebtedness and interest payments. In the planning of consumer goods production and retail turnover, and particularly the use of retail sales data and household budget survey data for demand projections, some attempt is made to allow quantitatively for the degree of shortage (*defitsitnost*) of a good. (15), (21).

[2] This applies also to producer goods to some extent. Soviet engineers and managers read the Western technical press. and this can create a demand for equipment and materials new to the USSR. In some areas of technology, of course, the flow can be the other way. For example, a Russian-designed relief valve with automatic oil-flow control for machine-tool transmission systems is described in *Machine Shop and Engineering Manufacture* (June 1969).

In the first category the products to which some advertising effort has been devoted are quite varied. They include several food products, notably Pacific fish, yoghurt and processed cheese; some durables, notably electric shavers, cine-cameras, transistor radios and knitting machines; household products such as detergents and electric lighters for gas stoves, and certain newly-expanded services such as laundries and dry cleaning.

The second category includes milk products and cheeses, for which there have been substantial multi-media campaigns; fruit compote and dried fruit; Georgian tea; cosmetics and perfumes; watches; motorcyles; savings bank services, insurance, rail and air travel.

Details of some of these cases will give some idea of what has been done and why. Supplies of Pacific fish have increased with the expansion of the Soviet fishing fleet. The expansion of meat supplies has, on the whole, been much less successful in the 1960s, and there has probably been deliberate policy emphasis on the development of fishing for that reason. However, many of the types of fish and crustaceans in the Pacific catch were new to most Russians. Relatively high prices (compared with those for familiar types of fish) have been set for some of them, and advertising emphasises their high nutritional value to overcome resistance to the price.

Yoghurt was produced by some diary concerns, apparently on their own initiative, without any initial marketing effort. In most areas it was previously unknown, and there are traditional Russian milk products which are close substitutes for it. Lack of sales led to its withdrawal from production by some dairies but in Estonia, especially, a press and television advertising campaign succeeded in creating a market, and production was expanded.[3] The 'Severyanka' knitting machine is quoted as a closely parallel case, with trade organisations clearing excess stocks of this formerly unknown product by press advertising which cost them less than one month's continued holding of the stocks would have done.[4]

[3] (27).
[4] (27).

(This was probably a small, once-for-all operation. There is no sign that Soviet women have been any more susceptible to knitting machines than women elsewhere).

In these cases, and also with the new detergents, e.g. Sintetika in the Baltic States,[5] there is a common sequence of events. A new product is developed and sold to distributors without any advance advertising to the general public by the producer. Retail and wholesale organisations, finding excess stocks on their hands, carry out some advertising, usually in local press, radio and television and usually at their own expense. Sometimes the producing enterprise is induced to share advertising costs.

Soviet writers on advertising press for preliminary marketing of new products by producers, but in conditions of general excess demand, and with some (varying, and not unlimited) scope for unloading output on the distributive system regardless of the latter's preferences, producers are not easily persuaded to incur marketing expenses, or at least not before they face the prospect of definite refusals of consignments on the part of trading organisations already holding excess stocks. One answer has been to introduce into the new 'model' trade-industry supply agreement a requirement that industrial suppliers should conduct preliminary advertising of new products.[6]

This requirement by itself is probably not very effective, like so many controls introduced to counter the unintended effects of other controls. It will tend to reinforce the disincentives to product innovation in Soviet industry. In market economies product innovation occurs in autonomous enterprises because — very broadly — it is a prerequisite for a desired rate of growth in sales and profits, and enterprise managers typically have strong incentives to expand sales and profits. The Soviet enterprise manager still does not seem to have strong incentives to initiate growth: he has incentives to respond to growth targest set from above, but his assortment, supply and other plans limit the means by which he can respond. Capacity limits make product innovation unattrac-

[5] (6), p. 31.
[6] (1), p. 8; (2), p. 81.

tive unless targets for other products are made less rigid. Risks of failure and costs of product development deter enterprises unless rewards for successful innovation are high.

The temporary raising of prices on new products is now allowed in order to meet the second requirement. However, in the West the market adjudicates between successful and unsuccessful product innovation, with appropriate effects on management incentives. In the Soviet economy there is often (though not always) insufficient feedback from final demand to the producers' financial incentives. So poorly selling new products or products that are minor variants of existing products, classified as new for pricing purposes but which consumers are not in fact prepared to pay more for, on a scale adequate to support continued production, can be unloaded on the distributive system at specially-raised 'new product' prices. The producer benefits from an 'innovation' which the market has not accepted, and distributors are faced with excess stocks. In some cases there is enough feedback from final demand to producers to penalise this sort of thing, but in many cases there is not. The present system seems unable, generally, to induce a marketing orientation in Soviet enterprises.

This might not matter if their superior ministry were so oriented. In fact product innovation often does stem from ministries and their divisions, via the research, development and design organisations, which are usually separate from individual enterprises and combines. But the ministry staff lack, with a few experimental exceptions, systematic pecuniary incentives to innovate. Outside the top priority sectors, their total incentive to innovate seems usually to be weak.[7]

On the other hand there is some genuine product innovation on the initiative of enterprises and ministries, especially in durables and other consumer goods originating in the traditional priority sectors, where the introduction of new products is in fact relatively rapid. The monthly *Novye tovary*, primarily for retail and wholesale staff, is a form of advertising of new products to distributors which gives some idea of the sort of new products being marketed.

[7] (33).

A breakdown of advertisements in the January 1970 issue is as follows (numbers of advertisements):

durables	9	
clothing, footwear, fabrics	4	(including one foreign advertiser
toys, musical instruments	4	
sports goods and other manufactured consumer goods	6	
food products	1	
producer goods	1	(including one foreign advertiser)

Individual items included television sets, a refrigerator, an electric juicer, an amplifier, a record-player, aqualung diving equipment, an electric guitar, a pedometer and children's anoraks.

The television quiz game 'Auktsion', mentioned earlier, has used expensive new durables as prizes. Such goods as cine-cameras have also been awarded to individual players in well publicised sports events, e.g. to the best player in a Spartak-Dynamo ice hockey match. Stadium announcers and television commentators were briefed to plug the products.[8]

Another category of new products that bulks large in local press advertising, and has tended to be the largest category of advertisements in the weekly supplement to *Vechernyaya Moskva*, is services. In the 1960s and early 1970s there was a policy of rapid development of the formerly neglected service activities of consumer-goods repairs, laundries, dry cleaning, public baths, hairdressing and photographic studios. Their total turnover rose by just under 63 per cent between 1965 and 1968.[9] New services and the new availability of old-established services have been quite strongly advertised.

The advertising of new products includes at least one case in which there seems to have been a centralised co-ordination of different sectors of a peculiarly Soviet type. With the

---

[8] (18). This was organised by STR and a specialist cine-camera distributive organisation.
[9] (39), p. 664.

large-scale introduction of gas supplies to housing in areas where it had previously been lacking, the increase in demand for matches, to light gas stoves and fires, outran that in supply capacity. Planners, possibly at republic level, asked producers of electric gas-stove lighters to increase output and were told that even at present levels of output excess stocks of lighters were already accumulating. Market research showed that few people knew what electric lighters were; an advertising campaign organised by RTR familiarised people with the product, sales rose and the problem is said to have been solved or at least diminished.[10]

In a Western economy the manufacturer of the lighters would probably have undertaken the market research himself; there is no special advantage in central co-ordination in this case. Central co-ordination in this instance replaces market mechanisms, and the initiation of market research and advertising differs accordingly.

It is for established goods in excess supply that multi-media, large-scale campaigns have been used. A Russian-republic campaign for milk products recruited well-known poets to write slogans and used television, cinema, radio and press. Fresh milk and some milk products are in short supply, but others are not. An intensive advertising campaign for cheese in Leningrad in 1968 aimed not only at raising the overall demand for cheese but at shifting demand from more to less established types. This campaign used several films, repeated daily on television over eleven days, and shown at cinemas, together with press and radio advertising, 100,000 leaflets and special shop displays, and it was preceded and followed by market research surveys. Campaign costs of 20,000 rubles were financed by a republic wholesale trade organisation and the city trade administration and organised by the latter's advertising department — not by one of the major advertising organisations.[11]

The advertising of 'sufficient' goods can bring obvious benefits from the points of view of planners, ministries and enterprises. In so far as it is successful, it absorbs some excess

[10] (23).
[11] (36).

demand by switching it away from *defitsitnyi* items. It also avoids or reduces costs associated with stock-holding, price-cutting and changes in output mix. Limits to its use for these purposes are set partly by the limits to the scope for selling absolutely anything by advertising. Thus for 1970 the major advertising organisations had planned to advertise only those television sets that were small, obsolescent and had accumulated in the shops, but in late spring prices on many of these models were roughly halved — a result which the advertising expenditure had probably been intended to avoid.

There are some indications, however, that advertising policy is also influenced by broader social considerations. Thus the campaign for milk and milk products not only used nutritional value as a selling point by may perhaps have been conceived partly out of the deliberate 'diet' policy associated with the rational consumption norms.[12] There is a minority opinion, apparently, among Soviet advertising people that some advertising of even scarce (*defitsitnyi*) items is desirable from a long-run, educational point of view.

Advertising of producer goods, i.e. advertising as part of industrial marketing, is of some, limited, importance. Technical periodicals in the West often consist to the extent of over fifty per cent, of advertising of equipment. These advertisements are a major source of technical information to specialists. The equivalent Soviet periodicals carry some advertising of this kind, but very much less, a substantial proportion of which is placed by foreign exporters. With some loosening of the administrative allocation of producer goods this advertising had tended to increase, but only a substantial further shift from allocation to market exchange would raise this advertising towards Western levels.

In all this advertising of different kinds of goods, what is the importance of branded goods and, more generally, of competition? Consumer durables are almost invariably branded, and fairly prominently so. Food goods are still sold without packaging to a substantial extent (73 per cent

---

[12] The RSFSR Ministry of Health and the USSR Academy of Medical Sciences, as well as the RSFSR Ministry of the Meat and Milk Industry, were involved in it. (29), p. 53.

in 1966 — see next section), and are therefore mostly anonymous. Where they are packaged the brand is usually that of the distributive organisation. Branding is not prominent in textiles and clothing or on many small household goods. It is however official policy to develop brand-marking, and has been so since the 1950s at least. State quality marks (awarded for conformity with 'the best international standards') are also used. Brand names therefore appear mainly but not exclusively in advertisements for durable goods.

Competition between close substitutes exists in some retail markets. The consumer can often choose between alternative branded versions of the same kind of goods in a given shop or within a given shopping area. This is true of durables, particularly, but also of, for example, the services of shops of a given kind in the same area. Recent Soviet market research has even concluded that there are too many models of televisions and perfumes on the market.[13] On the other hand, some branded items (for instance, sweets and chocolate in many places) are the only type available in a given area; i.e., the producers have regional product monopolies. And in many cases where different brands are supplied to a given area, or different shops offer similar services, there is at the same time overall excess demand for the good or service in question. So there is some brand advertising, but competitive pressure from other brands is not as a rule important.

Soviet official thinking favours branding but not competition. The producers of competing brands of a product will typically be subordinate to the same ministry and will certainly be subject to the same overall planning of output, supplies and other variables. While it is possible for manufacturing enterprises or combines to finance advertising up to some level from profits, the limits will not usually be very great. Approval of advertising expenditure of industrial enterprises by 'their' division in their superior ministry seems usually to be necessary. Their position in this as in other ways tends to be more like that of a subsidiary than a wholly independent company.

---

[13] (25); (26).

Competition between close substitutes other than branded varieties of a particular product is, of course, inevitable. There is some competitive advertising between Aeroflot and the railways, for example. Each has stressed in its advertising its supposed advantages over the other: safety as against speed, and so on. But this is exceptional and, as advertising wars go, it is a fairly quiet scuffle. It is possible that in inter-city travel, as in so many other Soviet markets, an overall excess demand takes the edge off any competition there may be.

Media-mix

The 1970 plans of STR and UTR give media breakdowns that are fairly detailed. Although they are plan, not actual, figures, they are apparently based largely if not entirely on orders and should correspond fairly well to the actual pattern of expenditure. Unfortunately they cannot be assumed to be representative. A large share of television advertising is channelled through these major advertising organisations, for example, while their share of press advertising is probably

TABLE 4.1 Media breakdowns for Soyuztorgreklama and Ukrto-
greklama, 1970 Plan ('000 rubles)

Media	STR	UTR	total
shop-window display equipment	1266	956	2222
printed matter (leaflets, catalogues etc.)	1805	2300	5373
press	1268		
cinema	150	234	1229
television and radio	845*		
neon lighting and repairs, etc.	4385	4448	8833
art work, fairs, other	813	2733	3546
	10,532	10,671	21,203

Source: interviews.
Note: In the STR column the 'television and radio' entry consists in fact of the following ('000 rubles): television films, 282; television transmissions, 298; television and radio announcements, 265; from which it is clear that television probably accounts for over 600,000 rubles of the total, and possibly for almost all of it.

much smaller, with trade and other organisations often dealing with the press. However, in conjunction with other information they do convey some notion of the relative importance of the main media.

The classifications used in the two media breakdowns differ for some entries. In table 4.1, therefore, some categories in each organisation's breakdown have been amalgamated to produce a category comparable to that available for the other organisation. The last column gives totals for the two organisations together.

These media breakdowns can be put into perspective by putting them beside Western data, though no precise comparison, of course, is possible. The STR breakdown is by categories that are closer than the UTR categories to the classification used in some Western data. Table 4.2 therefore compares the STR breakdown in percentages with an

TABLE 4.2 Advertising expenditure by media, STR 1970 plan and UK 1960

Media	STR (%)	UK (%)
shop-window display, etc.	12.0	5.5
outdoor*	41.6	6.2
catalogues, etc.	17.1	8.6
press	12.1	47.2
cinema	1.4	0.9
television**	8.0	17.7
other†	7.7	13.9
total‡	100	100

*neon, technical repair etc. only for STR
**for STR, includes radio
†for UK, includes radio, exhibitions, free gifts and samples and administration (STR administration costs are divided between media); for STR, includes outdoor other than neon; exhibitions.
‡the UK column does not add exactly to 100 because of rounding.
Sources: for STR table 4.1; for UK, Advertising Association estimates cited in Ralph Harris and Arthur Seldon, *Advertising and Society* (André Deutsch, 1962) p. 44.

approximately similar classification of UK national expenditure data for 1960. (The more recent 1964—8 estimates published by the Advertising Association are for advertising more narrowly defined.) It should be remembered that the quantities from which the percentages are derived are of an entirely different order in the two columns: the UK total is more than a hundred times larger than the STR total at the official exchange rate (which may be a very poor measure, but no other is available). Also, the categories used are only broadly, not exactly, comparable. The main differences incomparability that are known are indicated in the notes to the table. Exact knowledge of the contents of the STR categories would no doubt reveal other differences in coverage, but they should not be substantial.

Comparing the STR media mix with UK patterns is not in itself an illuminating exercise: STR will not be representative of the pattern of Soviet advertising in general. But we can make some allowance for this and then draw a few conclusions.

It was pointed out above that STR is very likely to handle a relatively large share of advertising. This is probably true also of cinema advertising. It appears, however, not to have a particularly large share of press advertising. On the other hand, catalogues, etc. are the largest category in advertising by industry,[14] and it is possible that for all Soviet advertising this medium is more important relatively to press advertising than it is for STR. The share of neon lighting and related advertising in the STR total is misleadingly high from the point of view of national patterns for two reasons: first, neon lighting is said to account for only 20 per cent of all retail and 5 per cent of all wholesale distributor spending on advertising,[15] second, much of the STR and indeed of all Soviet, expenditure on this medium is investment in intial installation of neon signs. The early development of the other

[14](1), p. 53. Advertising is said to occupy only about 8 per cent of the space in Soviet newspapers, and this no doubt includes film and theatre guides and small advertisements.
[15](2), p. 124. And advertising by industry and other producers is unlikely to have a very high concentration in neon lighting. In other words, STR specialises in this particular medium.

media is more in the nature of current expenditure. There-fore the share of expenditure on this item at present exaggerates its role in the current provision of advertising. The UTR breakdown is affected in the same way. On the other hand the 'outdoor' category in table 4.2 excludes posters, etc.

In Soviet advertising as a whole outdoor advertising probably plays a somewhat smaller role on balance than table 4.2 suggests, but one that is still large by UK standards. Catalogues, brochures, etc. probably bulk larger relatively to press, cinema and television than they do in the table.[16] In short, the overall pattern is almost certainly a rather 'old-fashioned' one, with outdoor advertising, shop-window display and catalogues, brochures and leaflets the leading media. The media which have for some time been the most important ones in developed Western countries — press and television — play only a small role.

To put it another way, the Soviet advertising media that are probably relatively least developed are press and tele-vision (and radio, compared with most Western countries other than Britian). The more 'old-fashioned' media are relatively more developed — though the difference from the West is still very large. One reason for this pattern is that outdoor advertising and shop-window display began to be developed in an earlier period, in part for purely decorative reasons. The arrangement of shop windows is often in fact carried out by a local authority 'decoration' agency and not by the shops.[17]

Packaging, too, is probably one of the relatively least developed media. Only 27 per cent of food goods (by value, presumably) were sold packaged in 1966. It was planned to raise this to 50 per cent by 1970.[18] Observation suggests that the percentage has been raised, but very probably not to 50 per cent over the country as a whole.

The role of the various media in Soviet domestic advertis-ing of domestic products is clearly very different from the

[16]. In the UTR breakdown the press and other printed matter item consists 'mostly' of the latter.
[17] (2), p. 126; (5), p. 87.
[18] (5), p. 70.

media mix for foreign exporters to the USSR. This is another indication of the entirely different nature of export marketing for this economy. Foreign advertisers concentrate their spending on the press (about 85 per cent) and particularly on technical journals (55 per cent).[19] There are two main reasons for the difference. First, consumer goods account for only a relatively small share of Soviet imports, while industrial equipment has a relatively large share. Technical journals are usually the best media for the latter. Second, even for consumer goods the usual target for the exporter is the major buying influence, not the final consumer. Direct contact, or possibly advertising to distributive trade managers in trade periodicals, may work with the former. The latter's influence on decisions to import is small, and for most imports, at present levels, his demand is ready-made. The position of the domestic advertiser is quite different.

Finance
The question of who initiates and controls advertising expenditure has already been partly answered in passing. The answers can be briefly summarised.

First, it is not at present 'the central planners' in any sense who initiate and control advertising expenditure. There is a central co-ordinating body for advertising (the IDCA) but it does not supervise or co-ordinate all advertising throughout the country. At present it quite possibly does not have much influence on the operations even of STR, RTR and UTR.

However, it is intended that some sort of central direction over Soviet advertising be developed. There seems to be little question of any attempt at detailed long-run planning of the advertising of particular products in the various media. Rather, the aim is to try to co-ordinate annual or possibly two-year plans of major campaigns, allocating responsibilities for financing between ministries, and to develop longer-run plans for the staffing and equipment of specialised advertising organisations concerned with agency and media work. In the special conditions of the Soviet economy it is probably desirable to have a strong central body to press the claims of

[19] (1), p. 54.

the advertising services sector for inputs. It has a low priority at present.

Advertising usually seems to be initiated at branch ministry level or below, usually without long advance planning, and financed in a fairly *ad hoc* way. The most typical process seems to be one originating within one of the Republic Ministries of Trade, and in particular from one of the wholesale product groups (*optovye kontory*) within a republic ministry. (The USSR Ministry of Trade has no wholesaling functions). These wholesaling organisations are responsible for the distribution of a particular group of products throughout a republic. Unlike almost all other Soviet organisations they have a regular but very small advertising appropriation (see chapter 3). They should also have better market information than other organisations, in the absence of specially-commissioned market research.[20] These organisations are usually concerned in any substantial advertising campaign, and advertising expenditure seems mostly to be decided on the basis of their information about sales, stocks and production. Both in the Leningrad cheese campaign and in a Yaroslavl campaign advertising fabrics,[21] the local trade administration and the Russian republic wholesale group were jointly responsible. The relatively new All-Union Institute of Market and Demand Research (VNIIKS) is directed more to more aggregated and longer-run planning of production and trade turnover and does not work closely with advertising organisations.

Cases in which the decision to advertise originates from an industrial ministry, combine or enterprise are less common. The Uglich watch factory regularly spends 20,000 rubles a year on advertising.[22] This small sum is mentioned approvingly as an example to other manufacturers. Attempts by STR to obtain finance from producer ministries and enterprises for advertising their new products, at least up to 1969, generally failed.[23]

---

[20] They sometimes do survey-type market research. (28). (32) describes market research by VNIIKS.
[21] (8), p. 144.
[22] (27).
[23] ibid.

As was explained above, the answer to this has been to impose obligations to finance advertising on industry, either through a high-level body, namely IDCA, or through the new model industry-trade supply contract or through a local-level Inter-Departmental Council on Advertising, such as the one at Gorky.[24] This has had the effect of increasing producer participation in advertising in some cases, but is likely to have reduced industry's incentive to product innovation (see above). STR apparently have more than fifty per cent of their orders from industry, but this probably refers to finance rather than initiation. UTR and RTR are working mainly for trade. Industrial initiative in incurring advertising expenditiure still seems largely to be confined to packaging, prospectuses, catalogues, etc. The Gorky IDCA succeeded in getting the local dairy industry to finance 60 per cent of a milk products campaign,[25] but such local councils cannot influence enterprises outside their areas and Gorky is exceptional so far in having such a council. Advertising expenditure in this council's area on products originating outside falls on trade.

There is still therefore a tendency for the old practice whereby 'industry produced the goods and . . . kept quiet'[26] to prevail. On the other hand, there is criticism of a purely financial role in advertising being allotted to producers — usually provided, apparently, by a rebate to distributive organisations to cover advertising.[27] It has been proposed that an explicit advertising appropriation be allowed for in industrial enterprises' costs, and that for large advertising campaigns on an All-Union scale there should be special earmarked advertising funds at ministry level in the various branches of production. Then industry would be responsible for the design and packaging end of the marketing mix and for marketing to distributors and to some extent to the population, while wholesaling organisations handled marketing to shops and most consumer display advertising.[28] This

[24] (96), p. 4.
[25] (29), p. 53.
[26] (5), p. 88.
[27] (31), p. 54.
[28] ibid; p. 57.

seems exceedingly rigid as a general scheme to be applied to different groups of products. Also, the more fundamental problem of motivation remains. The differences from the Western marketing balance between producers and distributors, even though the situation in Western countries is subject to some change, is apparent. Even in the early Kaldor-Silverman UK advertising data for 1938, the share of retailers was estimated at only 10 per cent.[29]

Ministries play a larger part than enterprises in marketing decisions. This is not too surprising, since ministries and/or their main divisions may be in many respects the Soviet version of the large corporation, or at least they may become so. It is the environment in which they operate, with central price and quantity controls, that makes the marketing situation so different from a Western one.

Content

What sort of social control is there on the content of Soviet advertising? The official principles of advertising policy have been outlined in chapter 2 above. The aims are said to be the education of people's tastes, the provision of information to consumers and the improvement of the service provided by distribution. Soviet advertising is supposed to be guided by ideology (i.e. by Marxism-Leninism), to be truthful, concrete, effective (in selling goods) and in conformity with plans.

Soviet advertising is said to differ fundamentally from Western advertising in its aims and economic functions, and hence in its content. An attempt will be made in the final section to reach some conclusions about the economic functions of Soviet advertising. From the point of view of content, what matters is that Soviet advertising tries to sell things that might not otherwise be bought. To this extent it cannot help but resemble Western advertising.

Its tone is none the less quite different. It is mostly inoffensive and unmemorable. The main reasons are obvious: first, the censor; second, the fact that Soviet advertising is

---

[29] Harris and Seldon, *Advertising and the Public*, p. 40. The more recent rise of distributors' brands is a different matter. The comparison intended here is with a period when industry in Britain is generally supposed to have had an old-fashioned lack of 'marketing orientation'.

only just beginning to develop. However, there may be other factors that are less obvious. One is the existence of an element of social policy in Soviet advertising, shown mainly in the propaganda for the so-called rational diet in the advertising of food products. It has already been mentioned[30] that the RSFSR Ministry of Health and the USSR Academy of Medical Sciences participated in the Russian Republic advertising campaign for milk in 1968. They may have done no more than provide information to be used as a selling point in the campaign. But if they did more than that, their involvement would indicate that the rational consumption norms do have some real influence on the content of advertising. Certainly, advertising of food products is apt to contain lists of vitamins and nutrients. Indeed, one Soviet advertising man has complained precisely that this often makes it ineffective.[31]

Whatever their origins, some of the limits on content at present are fairly clear. Soviet advertising specialists are mostly fairly familiar with the Western literature on advertising (though they tend to lack more direct experience of Western techniques). In commenting on it they take the line, not unknown in other spheres of Soviet life, that the West is a storehouse of useful techniques that can be put to better use (and used selectively) in a socialist context. Western studies of the effect on attention and memory of different kinds of advertising message, on different media, at varying intervals, and so on, are treated as valuable. But 'not all of the 800 ways of selling a good described in a recent foreign book are acceptable here and in line with our laws'.[32]

The approaches that are rejected are, for example, 'the constant use in bourgeois advertising of film stars and winners of all manner of beauty contests [*sic*] which is directed towards a feeling of philistine variety and mindless imitation.' On the other hand, to use a sports star to recommend a sports good, or a well-known technologist to recommend a piece of equipment would be entirely correct, since their opinions are authoritative.[33]

[30] n. 12 above.
[31] (96), p. 30.
[32] (5), p. 18.
[33] (22), p. 59.

'Penetrating to the very depths of the subconscious, winning over the consumer with arguments which may have nothing to do with the real consumer characteristics of the good, its usefulness' is the sort of thing that goes on only in the West. Motivational research is none the less still of interest in Soviet conditions because 'the scientific construction of the life of society has for the first time opened up possibilities for the scientific construction of man's inner life as well.[34]

Both in practice and in theory, therefore, there are limits on the kind of motives that can be appealed to. But in theory, at least, considerable sophistication of technique, using motivational research and other approaches, is possible. It is claimed that socialist advertising has loftier aims than its capitalist counterpart. It seeks to 'raise the culture of everyday life, introduce useful customs and traditions' [*sic*] and 'inculcate' (literally, 'graft on' or 'innoculate with') good taste. The motives of the advertisers therefore preclude the possibility of playing on the basest instincts of the advertisees,[35] whereas 'the advertising jungles of the capitalist West know no other master but money'. Competitive pressures lead Western advertisers to try to shout each other down, an escalatory process in which efforts at government control are 'like those of a solitary woodman against miles of tropical forest'.[36]

One does encounter slightly earthier views, particularly among practitioners. According to one senior editor, two or three years ago advertising people were fond of saying, ironically, that Soviet advertising was an unploughed field, with the implication that one could offer the Soviet consumer any sort of advertising material since he had not

---

[34] ibid. It was also pointed out in chapter 2 that non-figurative design in advertising, as elsewhere, is frowned on, and the principles of socialist realism appealed to. But the Soviet authors say there is not much use of pure abstration in Western advertising design despite the fact that abstract art is fashionable among the classes to which the advertisers belong, because such art is unintelligible and therefore ineffective in advertising. It looks as though Degtyarev and Kornilov, in (5), have discovered an interesting aesthetic principle which we might call capitalist realism.

[35] ibid.

[36] (5), p. 20.

been 'spoilt' by much advertising hitherto. This situation, the writer observed, would not last. He criticised vague and unconvincing advertisements with exaggerated claims, e.g. that the consumption of a fruit compote would ensure good health, and the amateurish use of unspecific terms, every kind of food product being described as 'tasty and nourishing'. He also criticised, as was mentioned above, advertisement overloaded with unintelligible nutritional terms. Advertising material, he quoted approvingly from an American author, must use one or at most two characteristics of a good; only a genius can use more and be effective. The 'useful kernel' of Western practice was for him its insistence on one or two key selling points. A better advertisement for fruit compote which he quoted was 'Open a jar of compote at dinner and the fragrant fruits of sunny Summer will bloom at your table.' [37]

In a similar vein, the commercial sponsorship of prizes in sports events, referred to earlier, has been defended against criticisms that it is not a technique that informs people about a good's 'real properties'. The writer argues that 'all that is needed is to catch [the consumer's] attention, leave an "image", inplant mini-information in his memory [*sic*]. He can get to know the good in the shop.' The same writer defends the television game 'Auktsion' against 'zealots of pure art who despise the advertising spirit' by arguing that the game serves a useful economic purpose. 'In the discussion of new forms of advertising, the [aesthetic] categories "good" and "bad" are out of place.'[38] Similar considerations of effectiveness affect shop-window display, where the view that it may be better not to show the prices of the most expensive things is not ruled out of court, though the traditional (and commendable) Soviet practice is always to price everything clearly.

In short, Soviet advertising is not immune to exaggeration and vagueness. It is also subject to technological imperatives, to borrow a phrase, that apply to other activities. The requirement of effectiveness conflicts in some degree with

[37] (9b). It sounds better in Russian.
[38] (18), pp. 53, 55.

that of pure information, and the latter is not likely to be rigidly insisted on. Whether it can conflict with that of truthfulness seems to depend on how narrowly 'the real characteristics' of products are defined, and there is no reason to think that the definition will be puritanical.

On the other hand, any substantial appeals to sex or status motives seem to be ruled out and to be likely to remain so unless Soviet society changes a great deal.[39] Outright falsification is likely to be at least as well guarded against as in other countries. Packaging (where it is used) and almost all labelling in shops is already excellent in giving information about weights, ingredients (so far as one can judge without chemical analysis) and prices. One safeguard is that in the last resort the 'image' that is at stake is that of the whole party and state system.

Conclusions

Most of the conclusions have already been suggested in this and the preceding chapter. To begin with, it is clear that the present volume of Soviet advertising expenditure is extremely small relative to Western levels. This is attributable to some extent but not primarily to the level of real household incomes: the major explanation lies in the nature of the economic system. The immediate influences are the prevalence of seller's markets, i.e. inflationary pressure repressed by price controls; the weakness of feedback from final demand to producers' incentives; the stringent financial position of the distributive system, and the relative weakness of the media's incentives to carry advertising. These are all, of course, connected with one another and are features of the economic system as a whole. The underlying trait of the system, to which they are connected, is the high degree of central control over prices and quantities.

On the other hand, Soviet advertising expenditure is almost certainly growing fairly rapidly. Further increase of income levels should maintain at least some growth. There is room for some disagreement about the trend rate of growth

---

[39] Soviet export advertising need not, and possible cannot afford to be, subject to quite the same constraints.

of real disposable personal incomes per head since 1965, but it has probably been of the order of four to six per cent per annum. Also, the long-run process of change of the system since the Stalin period (rather than the somewhat inconclusive 1965 reforms alone) is on the whole tending to strengthen incentives to incur marketing expenditure. There are, in particular, differences between markets, with more elements of competition and stronger feedbacks from final demand to producers in some branches than in others. The effectiveness of distributors' orders, and refusals of unwanted consignments, in influencing production plans is of key importance. Product innovation occurs, though rather weakly in many consumer branches, and is a factor leading to increasing expenditure on advertising.

On the whole, however, there remains a fundamental difference from market economies which will only be removed by more radical changes than have so far occurred. For the reasons already given, this difference in system leads to a substantially lower level of advertising in the Soviet economy, relative to consumption levels.

Soviet advertising is not notably subject to central control or co-ordination of the allocation of expenditure between products, media and places. Whether it will prove possible to make it so is questionable.

The incentive to advertise has so far been found mainly in the distributive system rather than amongst producers, and to a very substantial extent at republic-ministry and local trade administration rather than at enterprise level. To some extent the cost of advertising has recently been shifted rather more on to industry, but a general transfer of initiative to industry does not seem possible without substantial further changes in the whole system of planning and control. Greater enterprise autonomy as such, however, may not be necessary, or not in all branches. An increase in the autonomy of ministries, ministry divisions and/or large combines, implying an extension of market relations between them, may be enough to make production genuinely and generally 'market-oriented'. One major obstacle to radical change of this kind is that it would require either a successful macroeconomic control of disposable incomes, which is clearly not being achieved at present, or substantial de-control of prices while inflationary pressure continues, which is probably ruled out in view of the political consequences of deliberately allowing inflation to become open.

In the absence of changes of this kind, it is unlikely that Soviet advertising will approach Western levels (relative to total private consumption or GNP), or come closely to resemble Western patterns in its initiation.

While Soviet advertising is not at present subject to very much direct central economic control, it is not in any sense deliberately opposed by the central authorities. It is seen as assisting in raising private consumption levels, and the desirability of doing this is not questioned. On the other hand the advertising services sector is not at present given any priority, and the content of advertising is considerably constrained by policy. There is some evidence of a rather paternalist social policy influence on advertising, relating to the 'rational norms' of consumption, but whether this amounts to much in practice is not clear. The main function of advertising at present, is to introduce unfamiliar new products and to clear excess stocks of products where supply is tending to exceed demand at existing prices.

The question about the ultimate social use made of Soviet advertising at present therefore reduces to a question of the basis on which output decisions are made. On this there is little than can usefully be said except that the raising of consumption levels is one of the leadership's policy aims and that the understanding of what this means, both among the leadership and among the population at large, is very stronly conditioned by Western consumption levels and patterns. So far, therefore, it is hard to accept the official Soviet contention that consumer advertising in the Soviet economy serves a fundamentally different human purpose from consumer advertising in the West.

Soviet claims for the merits of (Soviet) advertising are in the last resort similar to those used in favour of advertising in the West, namely, that it serves only to realise latent needs and that the raising of consumption levels is a substantial good. The difference lies essentially in the substitution of central planned direction, in the Soviet case, for market mechanisms in relating production to consumption.

Another conclusion, which is perhaps a little more

interesting, though it is hardly surprising, is that Soviet experience does not show that socialised ownership of capital necessarily has much effect on incentives to advertise. Soviet producers and distributors already have some incentive to advertise, and the influences constraining advertising expenditure seem to stem from the system of control rather than that of ownership. The greater development of advertising in Hungary and Yugoslavia seem to confirm this.

It is to developments in Eastern Europe that we now turn. Conclusions based on comparison of Soviet advertising with that of decentralised socialist economies will be deferred until the final chapter.

APPENDIX TO CHAPTER 4

The rational consumption norms
The rational consumption norms are of considerable interest. The only extensive treatment of them in English that is known to me is in a PhD dissertation on the planning of consumption in the USSR by Phillip Weitzman (University of Michigan, Ann Arbor, 1969). What influence, if any, they have on actual planning decisions at present is uncertain. They consist of 'rational diet' norms for food products and rational consumption norms for manufactured products which are in many cases formulated as household stock norms (a 'rational wardrobe' of clothing, for example, and rational stocks of durables), and the overall result is a rational budget (for a given occupational group in a given area, etc.). The rational diet norms are said to be recommended by the USSR Academy of Medical Sciences Institute of Nutrition. How or by whom requirements in terms of nutrients are converted into requirements in terms of specific foodstuffs is not clear. A minimum-cost food budget satisfying a number of nutritional requirements is a standard linear programming exercise, but it is a little odd that this should be done by the Nutrition Institute, as it appears to be ((4), p. 171) and at the same time be influenced (for five-year projections) by production plans ((4), p. 170). Buzlyakov makes it clear that in five-year plans of production and retail sales there is some attempt to adjust planned supplies in the light of demand

TABLE A4.1   food norms (kilograms per head per year over the whole population)

	grain products	potatoes	vege- tables*	meat**	milk and milk products	eggs	fish	sugar	vege- table oil
norm	120.4	96.6	146	81.8	433.6	292	18.2	36.5	7.3
1968 actual as % of norm	128	136	54	59	66	49	72	102	89

*including melons
**including poultry, fat and all subproducts
†in terms of milk

projections based on household budget data and *also* in the light of the norms. He treats the norms as 'scientifically-based hypotheses' about what is desirable, which are not immutable. The original 'Khrushchev' norms have been changed ((4), pp. 171, 173), being raised for durables and lowered for most foodstuffs. A recent source ((10), p. 49) gives the data on food norms shown in Table A4.1.

Part II Eastern Europe

5 Relative income levels and differences in economic systems in Eastern Europe

To put the marketing situations in the various East European countries in context, it is necessary to have some idea of their relative levels of economic development, living standards and economic systems.

To begin with, overall economic development levels in Eastern Europe are below those of the UK or West Germany. Some East European countries, like Bulgaria and Romania, are at the semi-developed level of Spain or Greece. The conventional indicator is GNP per head, and a number of 'real' per capita GNP comparisons for the middle and late 1960s and for 1970 are given in appendix 1 to this chapter. That appendix also contains warnings about the low level of reliability of these comparisons, and it will be seen that some are mutually contradictory.[1] Statistical comparisons of 'real' GNP between countries are difficult and laborious to make. Their economic meaning — or, to put it more agressively, their human meaning — is often doubtful, especially between widely differing societies. They are at best a rather imprecise comparative measure of the total flows of goods and services produced.

---

[1] The contradictions are implied, rather than outright. Where the relation of one country's GNP or consumption level to another's is different in different tables in appendix 1 to this chapter, the comparison is for different years (e.g. DDR and Czechoslovakia in tables A5.2 and A5.3) or is on a basis that is not strictly comparable (e.g. USA and DDR in tables A5.3 and A5.4). However, changes in quantities and prices in each country over time suggest that these differences could not be fully explained by the differences in the years or price-basis of the comparisons.

The figures in appendix 1 to this chapter do, however, agree on some things that can be taken as meaningful and useful here. First, no Eastern European country closely approaches the UK, let alone the USA, in its overall level of economic development. Secondly, East Germany is the most developed (first equal, according to some figures), with Czechoslovakia close behind. Thirdly, Romania comes bottom of the Comecon class, with Yugoslavia somewhere around or below it. Finally, Hungary, Poland, Bulgaria and the USSR come somewhere between Czechoslovakia and Romania.

These GNP differences correspond roughly to differences in the degree of industrialisation, as indicated (inversely) by the share of agriculture in GNP and labour force. It is my impression that they also correspond roughly to the degree of technical sophistication over the whole range of industrial production, as observed by visiting Western engineers and businessmen. No country's branches of production all occupy the same position in this ranking as the overall national economy, of course. For instance, the Russians are some-where near the Americans in rocketry and way below the Yugoslavs (or at least the Croats) in consumer-goods packaging.

In average consumption levels the East—West differences are somewhat larger, and the ranking of the East European countries is somewhat different. The appendix gives some data on this but, as the comments there suggest, they are far from being precise and authoritative.

It should also be borne in mind that the figures in the appendix refer to average per capita personal or household expenditure only. For comparing different national market-ing environments this category is obviously important. It is widely believed that the level of advertising and promotion activity is related to the volume of discretionary household purchasing power, i.e. to the disposable personal income left after basic physical requirements have been met.[2] The more discretionary income there is, the more room for persuasion; hence, the more advertising and marketing expenditure relative to total consumer spending, other things equal.[3]

[2] For some workable definitions of discretionary consumption, and estimates of its growth in the USA in the post-war period, see George Katona, *The Mass-Consumption Society* (McGraw-Hill, 1964).

However, it is not clear what differences in advertising expenditure we should expect to find between East and West European countries purely as a result of differences in per capita private consumption levels. To begin with, the concepts of 'basic requirements' and 'discretionary income' are difficult to give a clear empirical meaning to, and even harder to use in international or inter-temporal comparisons. And historical data on advertising expenditure in Western countries do not go back far enough to reveal a period when this expenditure was substantially smaller relative to household spending than it is today. Evidence about relationships between consumption levels and advertising expenditure does not show a strong discretionary 'income' effect.

Moreover, the distribution of personal disposable income (or rather purchasing power, to take account of the effects of personal credit and wealth) is also relevant. There is no indisputable single definition of what is meant by a more or less even distribution of purchasing power, and the empirical evidence for personal income being more evenly distributed (in any sense) in socialist than in capitalist countries is less strong than one might expect. Still, it is almost certainly, on most definitions, somewhat more even.[4] This might be expected to affect levels and patterns of advertising expenditure.

---

[3] This proposition covers consumer-goods advertising but not, of course, all advertising. Growth in the advertising and promotion of producer goods and, arguably, 'personal' advertising (roughly, small ads.) expenditure must be differently explained.

[4] The only recent serious comparative East—West study of income distribution that is known to me is P.J.D. Wiles and Stefan Markowski, 'Income distribution under Communism and capitalism. Some facts about Poland, the UK, the USA and the USSR', *Soviet Studies* (January 1971 (part 1) and April 1971 (part 2)). There is, necessarily, a good deal of guesstimating in their comparisons. They find (part 2, pp. 505—7) that comparative wage and salary data for 1966 and 1967 show Poland and the UK to have relatively slightly more very low earners than the USSR, while the UK clearly has relatively rather more very high (wage and salary) income earners. However, the distribution of all net personal incomes, including incomes from capital, pensions, etc. and (in the USSR) collective farm peasant incomes, is another matter altogether, and from very poor data on both sides it is not clear that the average-income differential between the top and bottom five per cent of income units is less in the USSR than in the UK; the evidence suggests it may be similar (p. 508).

The extent to which free or subsidised state provision makes some kinds of personal expenditure unnecessary also has to be considered. This is also very hard to compare. Roughly, the importance of state provision of free health, education and welfare services, compared in aggregate monetary terms with personal consumption expenditure, is not markedly different in the USSR, and perhaps in the other Comecon countries, from its importance in the UK. It is almost certainly more important than in the USA. As for the relative importance of state-managed transfer incomes in total personal imcomes, the position seems to be roughly similar though comparison is very hard.[5] A major difference is that state housing subsidies in Eastern Europe are relatively very large. They have the effect of making housing expenditure a much smaller burden on the typical household budget (typically around five per cent, compared with around fifteen per cent in the UK). This is a less than splendid special achievement when you see how poor and crowded most people's housing conditions are in Eastern Europe. On the other hand, it does eliminate one source of financial worry for a lot of people, and leaves households with more discretionary purchasing power than a straight comparison of overall 'real' purchasing power would lead a Westerner to expect. It also makes comparisons of household budgets very difficult. It is one reason why the share of food, drink and tobacco expenditure in average household budgets seems so high (just under fifty per cent in Hungary in 1969, and not much less in the Soviet Union).[6] (The relatively low overall

[5] Wiles and Markowski, *Soviet Studies* (part 2, pp. 508, 509) find the relative size of public transfer payments in the USSR to be much larger than in the UK, but this is for the population excluding collective farm peasants. These peasants and their families were about 22 per cent of the Soviet population in 1969, were outside the social security system until the late 1960s, and still receive relatively small pensions and other direct benefits. Public transfer payments in the USA represent a smaller share of personal pre-tax income than in the UK (8 as against 10 per cent in 1968—9, according to T.E. Chester, 'America—A Reluctant Welfare State?' *National Westminster Bank Review* (February 1971) p. 34).
[6] (Hungarian) Central Statistical Office, *Hungary Today* (Budapest, 1970) p. 168. Food, drink and tobacco were 60.1 per cent of total

real income level and the distinctive retail price structure are also responsible. And in some of these countries heavy drinking is the national sport.) In short, expenditure patterns are different and not only because of differences in real income levels. One source of differences is the existence of repressed inflation.

In general, in those East European countries where centralised, Soviet-type economic management still prevails, there has in recent years been a tendency to repressed or partly repressed inflation in consumer-goods markets. To the extent that this inflationary pressure is repressed, i.e. that retail prices are held stable though demand exceeds supply at those prices, queues and shortages tend to develop or increase. This means the creation of a special kind of 'surplus' purchasing power which is quite unlike discretionary purchasing power in a market economy. There is plenty of money in people's pockets (or savings accounts) but no outlet for it. In those socialist countries where decentralised market allocation has been introduced on a substantial scale the situation is different.

This brings us to the question of how these economies are run. We will look first at Eastern Europe generally, and then separately and in more detail at the reforms in Poland, Hungary and Yugoslavia.

It is usually thought that there are two main criteria for distinguishing different systems in modern economies. One is the form of ownership of productive assets: broadly speaking, private, co-operative or state. The other is the form of control: are resources allocated by market relationships between independent units or by centralised administrative

---

Soviet retail purchases in 1969 (derived from the statistical yearbook *Narodnoe Khozyaistvo SSSR v 1969g.*, pp. 597 (collective-farm market sales), 606 (state and cooperative total and food and beverage sales) and 607 (tobacco sales). The addition of data for non-consumer retail sales, a very substantial rural subsistence production, other food supply channels, housing, services and other non-food expenditure might show that food, drink and tobacco were a somewhat lower proportion of total personal consumption, but their share would still be relatively high.

direction?[7] All real-life national economies have a mixture of ownership forms and methods of resource allocation.

All the East European economies are socialist in the sense that the larger part of their productive assets, output and labour force are in the state and co-operative sectors.[8] They vary, however, in the extent of their private-enterprise 'fringes'. They also vary in the extent to which the market mechanism is used to govern resource allocation. These differences are briefly summarised below for Poland, Hungary and Yugoslavia, with ownership details in appendix 2 to this chapter. The Soviet system was outlined in Part I.

One striking difference between the Soviet economy and some East European economies is that the latter have substantial legal private enterprise activities. In some cases they also have relatively independent and only very globally-planned co-operative enterprises.

Just how much this variation in forms of ownership affects the marketing situation is hard to say. It is the enterprises' relative autonomy, rather than their legal ownership forms, that is in my opinion important. Where they exist they tend to be part of an overall system in which market relationships are more, and detailed central planning less, important than in the USSR. Outside agriculture, private enterprise activities are generally rather of a fringe kind. The size of private enterprise units (e.g. floor-space of a shop), employment per firm and prices are generally subject to maxima imposed by the state. A limit of five non-family employees is usual. More than five employees are allowed in Yugoslavia, but taxation rates on private enterprises rise very steeply above that employment level.

In Yugoslavia agriculture is predominantly in private hands, though of course with large-scale state purchasing. Private enterprise is also substantial in handicraft and services activities. But in addition the system of workers' self-

---

[7] This is not an adequate basis for classifying modern economic systems, but it will just about do for our present purposes. The extent and nature of public and private sector interaction is important but hard to define in an operational way. I have discussed some of these issues in 'East—West Comparisons and Comparative Economic Systems', *Soviet Studies* (January 1971).

[8] See appendix 2 to this chapter.

management in industry, with (since 1965) substantial reliance on market relationships between units, is enough by itself to make the system radically different from any other in Eastern Europe. There is also some Western investment, with up to forty-nine per cent shares in joint production enterprises, and a very large volume of trade with Western countries, a large part of which is not subject to direct central control.[9]

In Poland also private agriculture predominates. But here there is a sharper division between a state-owned industrial sector with fairly detailed centralised allocation and a fringe of small-scale artisan, trade, catering and services activities which are controlled only in broad terms. A system of hiring out restaurants, for example, to private managers on a commission basis is one interesting experiment. Private entrepreneurs (outside agriculture) are licensed by the state and must renew their licences every two years.

In Hungary legal private enterprise activity appears to be relatively small in terms of sales or output shares (see appendix 2 to this chapter). There are none the less some 10,000 private retail traders, for example, many of whom are said to make relatively high incomes. Also, one feature of the post-1967 New Economic Mechanism is the encouragement of relatively autonomous co-operative organisations. These require formal licensing by a ministry but may be formed in various ways. The initiative can come from sources other than a ministry. These co-operatives are important in small-scale production and distribution, and several have developed in the fields of advertising and promotion. Spare-time private activity in repair work has also been institutionalised, with a legal licensing system, since 1969, but this is for craftsmen in full-time state employment. There are quite a few private shops, including over seven hundred in the clothing trade in 1969.

Let us now turn from ownership to methods of resource allocation. The classic Soviet-type centrally planned economy combines predominantly socialised ownership of resources with predominantly centralised administrative economic

[9] See *The Times* 'East—West Trade' supplement (19 May 1971) p. viii.

management.[10] It makes little use of the market mechanism
and has virtually no inter-enterprise competition. There is
now, however, a good deal of evidence that an economy can
combine socialised ownership of resources with substantial
use of the market mechanism and still work, by most criteria,
quite well. The extent to which the market mechanism is
used is—not surprisingly—very important so far as the role of
marketing is concerned. In my opinion it is far more
important than whether resource-ownership is 'socialised' or
private. It is, unfortunately, less easy to summarise.[11] What
is clear is that two of the countries considered here—Hungary
and Yugoslavia—are practising what might loosely be called
market socialism.

The extent to which the market mechanism is used means
the extent to which market relationships between independent units (farms, shops, enterprises or combines) determine
the allocation of resources. There are two dimensions to this.
One is the number and size of the sectors in which market
rather than administrative allocation is used. The other is the
proportion of major kinds of decisions, in any sector, that are
left to the market. What can the enterprise, combine, etc.
decide for itself? Total current output level? Product-mix?
Choice of inputs, choice of customers (including the choice

[10] The Soviet economy can be envisaged as a giant company with a very
high degree of centralisation, which has market relationships with
Soviet households (retail and labour markets) and foreign countries.
The 1965 reforms have not fundamentally changed this.
[11] One might try to construct an index of centralisation from, for
example, the number of instructions carrying financial rewards/
penalties received by enterprises, the percentage of retail and/or
wholesale turnover represented by products for which prices are not
centrally controlled, and the number of products whose allocation is
centrally controlled. But this will not work in practice for three
reasons. (a) The average or typical number of administrative orders
received by enterprises in practice is not reliably known. Polish sources
will admit to about eighty (J.G. Zielinski, 'On the Effectiveness of the
Polish Economic Reforms', *Soviet Studies* (January 1971) p. 415; most
Soviet discussion now speaks of eight or ten. This does not mean that
Polish industry is more centralised: it means that Polish discussion is
more honest. (b) The number of centrally allocated products is sensitive
to differences in the definition of products and of 'central allocation',
and its importance must be considered relative to total allocation,
which is difficult. (c) How is one to combine the separate indicators
into one index?

between home and foreign customers) and suppliers? Prices? Extension or reduction of capacity? Size and orientation of R and D spending? Whether or not to move into a completely different branch of production? And how much of its net income does the enterprise or combine dispose of, and under what constraints? What conditions and limits are there on its access to credit? In any given sector market relationships may be of very little importance, or they may determine current outputs and inputs with or without central authorities fixing the prices, or they may help to determine the pattern of investment. They may even help to determine the overall structure of the economy.

The extent to which the market mechanism is used is largely a function of the 'rights' of the business units. How many of the decisions listed above can they make for themselves? In all market economies the state sets rules within which markets operate, and appears as a buyer and seller on some markets. All market economies are in this sense 'managed' or 'guided'. Quality standards, general or selective credit control, monopoly policy, taxes and subsidies, prices controls and so on are all used to steer the decisions of 'independent' units in particular directions.

If the amount of market management could be quantified, it would almost certainly appear that the least managed market economy in Eastern Europe (presumably Yugoslavia) is more managed than the British market economy. Even the least centralised of these economies retains direct price, foreign trade and investment controls that are, or can easily be made, stronger than in Britain. The degree of decentralisation in Yugoslavia, however, is not clearly less than in, say, the French economy.

The other aspect of these countries' economic systems that is crucially important for marketing is the extent of sellers' markets, i.e. of queues and shortages at existing prices. This is closely related to, but not entirely determined by, the extent to which the market mechanism is used. It is not self-evident that detailed central administration of an economy must lead to a prevalence of sellers' markets. If planning were perfect, prices, quantities and incomes would be set so that markets were just cleared. In practice so far, centrally planned

economies have been subject to inflationary pressure, especially in consumer-goods markets. For good political reasons
their leaderships are reluctant to raise prices (consider the
Soviet food riots of 1962 and the Polish ones of late 1970),
so they have queues instead of open inflation.[1 2]

APPENDIXES TO CHAPTER 5

*1 Comparative GNP and consumption levels in Eastern
Europe, USA and UK*
A reasonable way of comparing development levels is to
compare per capita 'real' GNP, i.e. total production per head
of population in some common currency unit, with curren-
cies converted not at official exchange rates but at overall
(GNP) purchasing power parities.[1] However, reliable comparisons of this kind are difficult and laborious, and recent
ones are lacking for Eastern Europe.

Some short-cut methods have been tried out which in
essence amount to regressing a small number of readily
available national output or turnover data on comparable unit

---

[1 2] There is a cool discussion of queues versus price rises by the Soviet
economist Petrakov in the literary magazine *Novy Mir* (*New World*)
(August 1970) pp. 178—80. He observes that queues are common but
their 'nature and laws' have 'practically escaped consideration in our
economic literature'. He then gives the classic case against pervasive
administrative price controls: they turn consumption into a lottery, and
participation in lotteries should be voluntary. They also lead to bribery,
which is a concealed form of price increase, but with the addition of a
risk premium. He adds that the socialist law 'to each according to his
labour' is infringed because it is precisely people with time to spare for
shopping around who do best in a shortage situation. The Institute of
Economic Affairs, Milton Friedman and Adam Smith would strongly
approve. The egalitarian grounds for preferring queues to price rises are
stronger than he suggests, however, and the leadership-popularity
considerations are no doubt overwhelming. This article was singled out
for rebuke in *Pravda* (10 November 1971).
[1] W. Beckerman and R. Bacon, 'International Comparisons of Income
Levels', *Economic Journal*, September, 1966; F. Janossy, *A Gazdasagi
Fejlettseg Merhetosege es uj Meresi Modszere* (*The Measureability of
Economic Development and a Way of Measuring It*), Budapest, 1963; P.
J. D. Wiles (ed.), *The Prediction of Communist Economic Performance*,
Cambridge University Press, 1971, p. 381.

TABLE A5.1   GNP per head of population 1965 ($ at market prices)

East Germany	1629
Czechoslovakia	1629
USSR	1410/1290
Hungary	1140
Poland	1010/1182
Bulgaria	848
Romania	814

Source: P. J. D. Wiles (ed.), *The Prediction of Communist Economic Performance* (Cambridge: University Press, 1971) appendix, pp. 375, 377.

Note: These figures are themselves derived from estimates in a variety of sources, and the (very large) difficulties about them are explained in an extended note by Wiles, *The Prediction.*

TABLE A5.2   GNP per head of working population (ranking order)

1967 (Machowski estimate)	1969 (Stranski estimate)
1. East Germany	1. East Germany
2. Czechoslovakia	2. Czechoslovakia
3. Hungary	3. Hungary
4. Bulgaria	4. Bulgaria
5. Poland	5. USSR
6. USSR	6. Poland
7. Romania	7. Romania

Source: H. Machowski, 'The Degree of Integration of East German Foreign Trade in Comecon, 1971–1975', paper read to NASEES conference, London, April 1971.

Note: The Stranski estimate is presumed by Machowski to refer to 1969. In my opinion Machowski's ranking of USSR is too low, and would perhaps be more appropriate to consumption levels than to GNP. So, perhaps, is Stranski's. An estimate of GNP per head for 1967 by the UN Economic Commission for Europe, also cited by Machowski, puts the USSR in third place, above Hungary, Poland, Bulgaria and Romania (in that order).

'real' per capita GNP or consumption data for different countries, where the latter have already been compared by proper, full-blown purchasing-power-parity estimates. Comparative real GNP or consumption levels for other countries or other years, which have not been directly estimated, are then obtained by extrapolation.[2] I agree with the view that this seems to work poorly in comparisons between socialist and capitalist countries, but may work fairly well in comparisons between socialist countries.[3]

Here, then, are some comparisons for the middle and late 1960s, obtained from various sources and in various ways, which give a general picture of the relative level of development of East European economies. Not all of them agree, and the countries and years covered in each case are not always the same; but a rough ranking order can be seen, and some impression of the order of magnitude of differences between USA, UK and Eastern Europe can also be seen.

TABLE A5.3   GNP per head of population 1965 (in 1960 $US)

USA	2831
UK	1593
East Germany	1013
Czechoslovakia	890
Poland	660
Hungary	622
Bulgaria	552
Romania	507
Yugoslavia	442

Source: E. Erlich in *Kozgazdasagi Szemle* (*Economic Review*) (Budapest, 1970) no. 10, p. 1174.
Note: This comparison uses the Janossy method, one of the short-cut techniques mentioned above. For doubts on its reliability see Wiles, *The Prediction*, p. 381. If the omission of the USSR is intended to avoid giving offence (why else omit it?), it probably came out relatively low in this ranking (which covered thirty-two countries in all).

[2] Wiles, *The Prediction*, p. 381.

TABLE A5.4   GNP per head of population, 1965 (East Germany = 100)

USA	227
East Germany	100
Czechoslovakia	100
USSR	86
Hungary	70
Poland	62
Bulgaria	52
Romania	50

Source: Joint Economic Committee, US Congress, *Soviet Economic Performance 1966—67* (Washington, 1968) pp. 12, 16, 119, as cited by Wiles, *The Prediction*, p. 389, with US figure added by Wiles.

TABLE A5.5   GNP at market prices per head of population, 1970 (in $US at 1969 prices)

USA	4530
France	3400
West Germany	2960
Italy	1930
UK	2540
USSR	2090
Bulgaria	1310
Czechoslovakia	2130
East Germany	2200
Hungary	1460
Poland	1350
Romania	1140

Sources: Derived from national official data for mid-1970 population; GNP estimates for all except USSR from CIA unclassified material; USSR: GNP derived as median of several Western estimates of Soviet GNP as a percentage of US, 1967—70, applied to US 1970 GNP figure at 1969 prices.

Here are some comparisons of household consumption levels.

TABLE A5.6   Per capita personal consumption, 1965 (in 1960 $US)

USA	1520
UK	1047
East Germany	563
Czechoslovakia	513
Hungary	401
Poland	362
Bulgaria	347
Yugoslavia	302
Romania	268

Source and method: as table A5.3.

Table A5.6 is based on one of the short-cut methods (see above), whereas table A5.7 is a direct purchasing power parity (p.p.p.) comparison. It is therefore likely that the East European countries appear in table A5.6 to have rather lower consumption levels relative to Western countries, than a proper p.p.p. comparison would show. For this reason, Soviet 'real' consumption levels should probably be inserted lower down in the ranking order of table A5.6 than a comparison of tables A5.6 and A5.7 would suggest.

TABLE A5.7   Per capita personal consumption, 1965 (USSR as % of UK)

(a)	with purchasing power parity as average weighted by Soviet expenditure patterns	60
(b)	with purchasing power parity as average weighted by British expenditure patterns	40

Source: P. Hanson, *The Consumer in the Soviet Economy* (Macmillan, 1968) p. 59 (revised estimate for (b)).

At the same time, if we stand back a bit from the technicalities we will see that table A5.6 may not really understate East European average consumption levels in comparison with US and UK levels (for the mid-1960s). This is because the 'proper', conventional p.p.p. statistical comparisons compare the purchasing power of the ruble or zloty to that of the pound or dollar without allowing for the poorer quality, range and availability of goods and services in the socialist countries. We know that these differences are real, important and large, but nobody has yet found out how to quantify quality (over the whole range of goods and services) or how to measure availability. It is true that for some countries this problem is becoming less important. In Hungary and Yugoslavia, especially, the quality and availability of goods have in recent years come closer to West European levels. By the same token, statistical comparisons between these and other East European countries are in this respect becoming more difficult, and I would regard table A5.6 as a rather poor guide to relative consumer well-being in different East European countries today.

In general, none of these figures is more than a very rough indicator.

Relative importance of state, co-operative and private enterprise

The official national statistics of the USSR, Poland, Hungary and Yugoslavia give various data indicating the relative importance of different forms of ownership in these economies. Most of the data are not precisely comparable between countries, since coverage and definitions vary. All, of course, exclude illegal activities. Table A5.8 has been calculated from these sources. Definitions and sources are given below. It should be borne in mind that the word 'co-operative' means different things in different contexts. In Soviet agriculture it means collective farms very closely controlled by state and party. In Polish, Hungarian and Yugoslav industry it means relatively autonomous and loosely-supervised small organisations.

TABLE A5.8   Percentage shares of state, co-operative and private
enterprise in major economic sectors, 1968 or 1969

sector	USSR	Poland	Hungary	Yugoslavia
industry (a)				
state	99.8	89.6	93.2	97.1
co-operative	0.2	10.0	5.6	
private	0.0	0.4	1.2	2.9
agriculture (b)				
state	(38)	15.0	15.5	20.5
co-operative	(50)	1.2	73.0	
private	(12)	83.8	11.5	79.5
retail trade (c)				
state	68.3	47.8	66.4	
co-operative	28.9	50.8	32.8	n.a.
private	2.8	1.3	0.8	

Notes:

(a) Industry

> *USSR:* gross industrial production, 1968, at current prices. Including mining; excluding construction. Construction is carried out by state organisations, with the exception of (largely rural) house-building by collective farms and private households. The tiny share of co-operative industrial production consists of the net off-farm sales of the recently developed subsidiary industrial enterprises of collective farms. An estimate of these is given in a recent Soviet article, and I have added it to the official total for industrial production.

> *Poland:* gross industrial production, 1969, at 1960 prices. Including mining, excluding construction and industrial-type craft production. Co-operatives are of two kinds: craft (excluded here) and factory, in which latter there is joint ownership. The private sector accounted for 12.4 per cent of gross production in construction. Data on the production of the (private) craft workshops are lacking, but numbers engaged in it in 1968 were 5.2 per cent of total numbers engaged in industry. The state administration is said to have applied a squeeze to the private supplies of producer goods and services in 1969–70 in order to divert private activity to consumer services. *Zycie gospodarcze* (7 February 1971) pp. 6–7, as cited in *ABSEES* (July 1971) p. 237.

Hungary: gross industrial production, 1969, current prices, including mining, excluding construction. The private sector accounted for 11.0 per cent and the co-operative sector for 17.4 per cent of gross production in construction.

Yugoslavia: net national material product originating in industry, 1968, current prices. Including mining, excluding construction and craft production. No division between state and co-operative activities is given; ultimate formal control usually rests with producer co-operatives (workers' self-management). In construction the private sector accounted for 14.5 per cent of net national material product. If the large, and predominantly private, handicraft sector is added to the 'industry' total, the private share would rise to 8.7 per cent.

(b) For agriculture data are often lacking on shares in total production in value terms.

USSR: shares in off-farm sales, 1969, at current prices. These exclude all intra-rural sales not involving state purchasing agencies. In view of the large extent of rural subsistence production from private plots, and no doubt some intra-rural trade in private-plot produce, these figures seriously understate the importance of private agriculture in total Soviet food supply. A recent Soviet source puts its share in gross agricultural production at about one-third (see *ABSEES* (July 1971) p. 125). In 1969 the private plots accounted for the following percentages of total production in physical terms: grain, 2; potatoes, 67; vegetables, 39; meat, 35; eggs, 56; wool, 21.

Poland: total agricultural land-use shares in mid-1969. 'Co-operative' here refers to what are officially classified as type III and type IV collective farms, and 'private' to types I and II collectives. It can be argued that type III collectives and sub-type IV (3) are also still in practice groups of private peasant smallholders with little sharing of inputs or revenue. For an explanation of the types, see Andrew Elias, 'Magnitude and Distribution of the Labor Force in Eastern Europe', in *Economic Development in Countries of Eastern Europe* (US Congress, Joint Economic Committee: Washington, 1970), esp. pp. 172—3 and 179.

Hungary: gross agricultural production, 1969, at current prices.

Yugoslavia: net national material product originating in agriculture, 1968, current prices.

(c) Retail turnover, including catering, 1969, current prices.

   USSR the figures are for the share of peasant markets in total retail sales. These exclude intra-rural peasant trade but include some sales by collective farms on urban markets.

   Poland: some categories of private trade are excluded, so the private share is understated.

Sources:

   USSR: The statistical yearbook, *Narodnoe khozyaistvo SSSR v 1969g.* (Moscow, 1970), pp. 297 (shares in off-farm sales of agricultural produce), 295 (shares in agricultural production, in physical terms of different product groups) and 600 (retail trade shares). Industrial gross output from p. 143, with collective-farm subsidiary enterprise data from *Voprosy Ekonomiki*, no. 8 (1970) p. 136.

   Poland: The short (but still very detailed) statistical yearbook (Russian-language version), *Kratkii statisticheskii yezhegodnik PNR 1970* (Warsaw, 1970), pp. 91 (industrial production shares), 87, 110 and 140 (definitions, total industrial employment, numbers engaged in private industrial-type craft work), 145 (construction shares), 157—60 (agricultural ownership-sector definitions), 166 (land-use shares) and 225, 227 (retail sales: definitions and data).

   Hungary: (Hungarian) Central Statistical Office, *Hungary Today* (Budapest, 1970) inside front cover.

   Yugoslavia: Statisticki godisnjak Jugoslavije 1970 (Belgrade, 1970) p. 104 (industrial, agricultural, construction and handicraft data).

6 The marketing environment

Poland

The Polish economy remains, as was said above, fairly close to the Soviet economy in organisation and control. In other words, it is still highly centralised. The production enterprises still stand, as one Polish economist put it to me, 'with their backs to the consumer and their faces to the plan'. So far as the domestic economy is concerned, there has not been a radical economic reform. There has however been, in the best Polish traditions, plenty of interesting discussion of economic reform. The allocation of information and ideas, at least, is quite decentralised.

The number of instructions handed down to state production enterprises is still large, and still covers the main aspects of their work. There has been an interesting development, however, of associations of state enterprises. These are in composition closer to large multi-plant firms than the Soviet-style branch ministry and its empire, and they have taken over some functions from the Ministries. They control their own research and development institutes, for example, as well as much of the more detailed production and investment decisions. One important change is that industrial associations generally have taken over (from the Ministry of Foreign Trade) those foreign trade organisations that deal in 'their' range of products. According to some Polish economists there should be a further development towards a set of Galbraithian state-industrial complexes. In some branches an intermediate unit, which we might translate as 'combine', has been developed between enterprises and association level. It typically groups several enterprises under a 'leading enterprise' as in one form of the Soviet *ob"edinenie*. For the time being, however, centralised control over the associations remains fairly detailed. One specialist on the Polish economy

95

considers that there has been confusion between decentralisation to association level and decentralisation to enterprise
level.[1] Clearly you cannot — generally and simultaneously —
have both. The parts of the economy that are not strongly
centralised are the private and small-scale co-operative sectors
mentioned above. These do contribute some competition and
market-orientation in some sectors.[2]

The important organisational differences from the Soviet
marketing environment are in my opinion two. First, the
foreign trade reforms. In general, the Polish economy has
been made more open to foreign trade, with the aim of
gaining more from it via greater internal competition and
competition of Polish products on world markets. This is
expected to lead to technical and quality improvements in
Polish production, as well as the classical gains from trade.
The shifting of some foreign trade organisations to the
industrial associations has already been mentioned. In addition some enterprises can now import on their own
initiative, dealing directly with foreign firms, in amounts
determined by their own export earnings. Some can engage
directly in foreign barter deals — the large Centrum department store among them. Domestic price reforms have aimed
at aligning the Polish domestic price structure more closely
with world market prices. Prices in foreign transactions are
translated into zlotys at single, uniform rates (40 zl = 1 ruble,
60 zl = $1). These are not the official exchange rates, nor are
they necessarily rates at which the balance of payments
would tend to long-run equilibrium if foreign transactions
were completely decontrolled.[3] But these changes together

---

[1] Zielinski, *op. cit.*, (ch. 5, n. 11) p. 425.
[2] The decision by the Gierek leadership to remove compulsory delivery
requirements from the private peasants (from 1972) and to encourage
some of them (financially) to expand their holdings should strengthen
the responsiveness of agriculture to consumer demand by facilitating
greater specialisation on individual holdings. See the article by Richard
Davy in *The Times* (25 June 1971) p. 12.
[3] The idea is to set rates at which the flow of exports desired on balance
of payments grounds can be maintained at competitive foreign-currency
prices, while keeping considerable central control over the levels of
imports.

enable a more rational choice of import and export items and volumes to be made, and remove the cross-subsidisation of products in the foreign trade system. It should also be noted that there is some production of Western products under licence, e.g. the Polish Fiat.

Altogether, there is more openness to products from convertible-currency (i.e. 'Western') countries than in the USSR. Competition from Western products in the home market, however limited, and competition in Western markets seem to be more of an influence on Polish than on Soviet marketing.

The other difference from the Soviet Union is that the sellers' market in consumer goods is less marked. In the March 1971 wholesale fair a large number of internal trade organisations refused for the first time to enter into purchasing contracts for a substantial number of the consumer products displayed.[4] This sort of thing can and does happen in the Soviet consumer sector, but so far only on a small scale. In this situation it becomes harder for industrial managers to earn bonuses without regard for market demand, and they are almost certainly being forced to become more market-oriented than their Soviet counterparts. Such changes can come about, as the chapters on Soviet advertising tried to show, even in a system where detailed central administrative allocation remains. The process seems to have gone further in Poland than in the Soviet Union.

The small private and co-operative fringe activities also contribute to the easing of the sellers' market by plugging gaps in supply, particularly for the heart-warming trivia which the Soviet-type economy seems to be quite hopeless at supplying, like big, round, silver-rimmed sun glasses and steak Chateaubriand in candle-lit restaurants.[5]

Since all modern industrial economies in the post-war period have usually experienced inflationary pressure, the

---

[4] Information from interviews.

[5] Appendix 2 to chapter 5 gives data on the quantitative importance of the private sector. What is asserted here is that its role in raising product quality and in innovation is almost certainly larger.

main alternative to queues, shortages and sellers' markets (repressed inflation) is price increases (open inflation). [6] The fact that Polish retail prices have tended to rise in the late 1960s (quite apart from the special increases of late 1970 which caused so much trouble) probably indicates that the Polish economy has tended to have more open inflation of retail prices and has therefore been somewhat less prone to shortages and sellers' markets than the Soviet economy. Most prices remain, of course, state-controlled.

TABLE 6.1 Polish indexes of retail prices (previous year = 100)

	1965	1966	1967	1968	1969
all goods and services	100.9	101.2	101.5	101.5	101.2
goods in state and co-operative trade only	100.3	100.6	100.99	101.1	100.8
food products in urban free markets	104.0	95.3	104.8	103.0	107.6
services	102.1	108.1	102.8	102.7	100.2

Source: Kratkii statisticheskii yezhegodnik PNR (Short statistical handbook of the Polish People's Republic — in Russian) (1970) pp. 340, 341, 342.

Hungary
The Hungarian economy is the prime example of a formerly Soviet-type economy that has decentralised its economic decision-making. [7] It is at present the only Comecon country

[6] This is of course an over-simplification. It is possible to have 'concealed open' inflation, i.e. quality decline at constant prices, or a change in the quality-mix of products sold which has the effect of making the average cost of product X, widely defined, higher without affecting official price indexes, and bribery (note 12 to chapter 5 above). It is often asserted that such changes are substantial and frequent in East European markets. I doubt this, but in any case it is clearly an oversimplification to say merely that prices remain constant and shortages appear or increase in conditions of repressed inflation.
[7] Yugoslavia began to do so soon after it broke from the Soviet bloc in 1948, but it had scarcely had time to become a completely Soviet-type economy to begin with.

in which the market mechanism has substantially replaced detailed central administration in domestic production and distribution. The reforms were introduced in one big package on New Year's Day, 1968. However, though the introduction was abrupt, the prior preparation was prolonged and meticulous, with specialists (including practitioners as well as mere academics — though in Hungary the two occupations are often combined) in many fields writing papers on reform measures in their own branches and discussing and dovetailing detailed proposals for change. Marketing was one such field. The relative calm in which the reforms were worked out is unique in communist experience, and their thoroughness and soundness has no precedent. There was no external political crisis, as when Yugoslavia broke with the Soviet Union, and no acute problem of falling growth rates, as in Czechoslovakia in the early 1960s.

The reforms are well described in detail (in English) in a recent Hungarian book.[8] So far as the marketing environment is concerned, the main features of the New Economic Mechanism can be rather crudely summarised as follows. Enterprises now receive no detailed instructions from above. They make their own output, input, supply, disposal, product-mix and investment decisions with a framework set by the central authorities. Their basic incentive comes from profits. The government, like governments elsewhere, takes a part of net profits, leaving about 40 per cent to be retained by the enterprise. It also sets some price ceilings, sets limits to the allowable annual increase for some prices and leaves other prices completely free (initially covering 50, 27 and 23 per cent respectively of retail sales, with the 'free' category rising to 29 per cent in 1970; many producer-goods prices are completely free). It also sets rules governing the allocation of retained net income as between bonuses for various categories of staff, and investment. Hence, and through other rules (recently strengthened), there is an attempt at direct control of personal incomes for macroeconomic stability.

In this situation the industrial ministries concentrate more

---

[8] I. Friss (ed.), *The Reform of the Economic Mechanism in Hungary*, (Budapest: Akademiai Kiado, 1969).

on the provision of information and consultation and some
support in the activities of risk-taking and R and D. They also
have the power to found, liquidate and amalgamate enterprises, to hire and fire executives and to set limits to the
sphere of operation of the enterprise. In practice so far, it
seems that these are usually reserve powers. Enterprises,
jointly or singly, and local authorities can also form new
enterprises. These and co-operative ventures are, it appears,
normally given licences more or less automatically by the
relevant ministry. Senior management incomes may be
substantially affected by enterprise profits and losses (whereas other employees have almost all their incomes guaranteed),
and the aim is to encourage entrepreneurship while keeping
state ownership of capital.

The major structural changes in the economy and social
infrastructure are supposed to be determined by centralised,
budget-financed investment. Some, but only a little, centralised materials allocation has been retained. Foreign trade is
controlled by a mixture of quotas, import deposits, licences,
exchange-rate control and (in special circumstances) direct
instructions. About ninety Hungarian firms are able to deal
directly with foreign buyers or sellers.[9] Licencing agreements
with Western firms and (recently) co-ownership arrangements
in production, provided there is majority national ownership,
has been allowed. According to a recent source, 151 such
agreements had been signed with Western firms by the end of
1971.[10]

Because of these changes, many of the features of a
Western marketing situation have appeared. There is already
some price and product competition, and it appears to be
growing. Curiously enough, a pre-communist, indeed 1920s,
law on competition has recently been invoked in legal
disputes over 'unfair' competition. Western goods have been
imported on a large scale, deliberately, to stimulate such

[9] Professor I. Szasz, Head of the Law Department of the Hungarian
Ministry of Foreign Trade, speaking at Birmingham Chamber of
Commerce on 23 November 1972. This figure excludes the 28
specialist foreign trade companies.
[10] Dr T. Palagyi of Danubia Patent Bureau, speaking at Birmingham
Chamber of Commerce on 23 November 1972.

competition. A single exchange rate is used to convert foreign-trade prices into domestic currency, as in Poland and indeed with the same rates for the forint as for the zloty. By East European standards a large proportion of imports have been consumer goods. About 23 per cent of retail sales of non-food goods in 1970 consisted of imports.[11] A large proportion of these were from the West. Typically these have been things no puritan would classify as prime necessities. Perhaps they are psychological prime necessities though.[12] Coke, Pepsi, Ronson, Helena Rubinstein, Dior, etc. are now conspicuous in Budapest shops and advertisements. More important in the long run, in my opinion, is the freedom of domestic enterprises to innovate and change their product-mix.

The shift away from Soviet-style shortages and sellers' markets is not so far complete, however. Retail price controls have of course been maintained on 'necessities', with free prices being mainly for 'luxury' items. According to the Hungarian Marketing Institute, the main market research organisation (which among other things publishes frequent and detailed bulletins giving supply capacities, prices, known demand and product specifications for a wide range of goods), the quantity, quality and assortment of supplies in early 1971 was generally in balance with demand at existing prices for food (except beef), and textiles, but for other manufactured consumer goods there were shortages at existing prices for particular qualities and varieties of product, though overall supply by product group roughly matched demand in monetary terms.[13] Anyone who arrived in early 1971 in Budapest from Moscow, once he had got

---

[11] Information from interviews.

[12] The allure of Western consumer goods to East European consumers is hard for a Westerner with no experience of these countries to grasp fully. I have tried to convey the feel of the situation in Moscow in 'Acquisitive Dissent', *New Society* (29 October 1970), reprinted in Paul Barker (ed.), *One for Sorrow, Two for Joy: Ten Years of New Society* (Allen & Unwin, 1972). The more such goods are available, the less intense is the allure, so that people are more relaxed about such things in Warsaw, and still more so in Budapest. Californian middle-class drop-outs are just a bit farther along the line.

[13] Therefore, presumably, there were also surpluses of some products within major product groups.

over his initial euphoria, would still have found, if he looked closely and long enough, some queues. Partly as a corollary of this, and partly as a result of good macroeconomic planning and control, the rise in retail prices since the introduction of the New Economic Mechanism has been small. Those prices that were to be freed under the New Economic Mechanism were reduced just before the reforms were introduced, so their upward movement in 1968 left the overall consumer price index unchanged over 1967. The workers' and employees' price index has since risen at around one per cent per annum and the peasants' consumer price index rose by two per cent in 1969. The overall increase in the consumer price index from the introduction of the reforms through 1971 was only about 3 per cent. Meanwhile national income (net material product) has been rising at about 5½ per cent per annum.[14]

Yugoslavia
The Yugoslav economy defies succinct description by a non-specialist. I personally rather doubt whether specialists understand it either, and that includes Yugoslav specialists. The precise roles in economic decision-making of the party leadership, the federal, republic and commune government bodies, the enterprise workers' councils and enterprise directors are hard to establish. There is some disagreement about how the system works at any time, and in addition the formal balance of powers has been changed in frequent reforms. During 1971 a combination of economic and political problems made the survival of the existing system seem somewhat precarious.

What is clear is that the market mechanism is extensively used, especially since the reforms of 1965. The extent of private enterprise activity is shown in appendix 2 to chapter 5. The socialist sector consists largely of enterprises that are legally state-owned but legally controlled by their own workers via the workers' councils, which now select the enterprise director, supervise the share-out of salaries and wages and should in principle be consulted on major policy

---

[14] *Statistical Pocketbook of Hungary 1972* (Budapest, 1972) pp. 70 and 237. The overall success, however, of the NEM remains (in 1973) open to question.

issues. It appears to be relatively easy to set up a new enterprise provided you play by the workers' self-management rules. The enterprise normally has a great deal of independence in all current production decisions. A high overall rate of investment used to be ensured via enterprise allocations of profit to federal and republic budgets, and centrally-determined rules on the allocation of retained net revenue between workers' (and managers') incomes and investment. The 1965 reforms, however, abolished direct taxation of enterprise income (i.e. gross revenue *less* material costs and depreciation). Enterprises have since retained about 70 per cent of income (capital charges and turnover tax accounting for the other 30) and direct control of the allocation of that 70 per cent between workers' incomes and re-investment has been removed. The result has been inflationary rises in personal incomes, though the share of fixed investment in GNP (see references at footnote 15) does not seem to have declined. It appears that the state authorities normally have no control over how an enterprise invests its retained profits, but control over credit, through the banking system, is considerable. Therefore, as in Hungary, the pattern of investment is not (in principle, at least) substantially surrendered to the market.

Market socialism has a longer history in Yugoslavia than in Hungary. The market probably also has a larger role in some respects. About 50 per cent of imports are free of controls. In 1968, 66 per cent of retail and 56 per cent of wholesale prices were not subject to controls.[15] Perhaps the clearest indication that Yugoslavia is in a very real sense a market economy is that it suffers from market-economy ailments: inflation, unemployment, balance of payments problems and business illiquidity. The cost of living index rose by over 20 per cent between 1965 and 1966, at about 6 per cent per annum for the following two years, and then by 8 per cent between 1968 and 1969.[16] In the first four months of 1971

---

[15] *Ekonomska Politika* (7 December 1970) pp. 13—14 as cited in *ABSEES*, (Soviet and East European Abstracts Series) National Association for Soviet and East European Studies, 1971) p. 248.
[16] *Statisticki godisnjak Jugoslavije 1970* (*Statistical Yearbook of Yugoslavia 1970*) (Belgrade, 1970) p. 259.

the index was about 13 per cent above the corresponding period of 1970,[17] and this despite a price freeze imposed in 1970.[18] To a considerable extent the unemployment problem has been exported, with about 900,000 Yugoslavs working abroad by the end of 1970.[19] It has been estimated that in 1970 about one in every eight enterprises made a loss. Visible imports in the first four months of 1971 were about twice as high as exports.[20]

Despite (and also because of) all these market-economy symptoms, direct state intervention is far more frequent in the Yugoslav than in most Western economies, according to Yugoslav managers I spoke to. A recent example was an enterprise that was instructed at short notice to re-direct a large part of its planned exports from Western to Soviet markets. This required substantial changes in the product. Western exporters to Yugoslavia cannot generally be sure of retaining their place in the market from year to year because of such *ad hoc* intervention. This sort of thing, I was told, also makes long-run enterprise planning more difficult for Yugoslav enterprises than it would be in a Western market economy. In general it is a feature of all socialist economies that enterprises have a less stable environment than Western firms for this reason. Even the 'market socialist' countries have not yet changed this situation, though I see no reason why they should not do so eventually. The effects of this on marketing are obvious. However, Western firms whose products are made in Yugoslavia under licence can now direct their own marketing policy there. Such firms were believed to do more advertising and marketing, as a rule, than foreign exporters (which suggests that the planning of domestic enterprises is far less uncertain than that of foreign exporters to the Yugoslav market). This has had a considerable influence on domestic Yugoslav marketing.[21]

[17] *Borba* (Zagreb edition) (6 May 1971) p. 8.
[18] *Privredni vjesnik* (*Economic Herald*) (5 November 1970) pp. 1, 2, as cited in *ABSEES* (January 1971) p. 245.
[19] Figures ranging from 850,000 to one million are quoted from various Yugoslav sources in *ABSEES* (April 1971) pp. 247, 251.
[20] *Borba* (Zagreb edition) (6 May 1971) p. 8.
[21] The production of Coca-Cola and Pepsi-Cola under licence in Yugoslavia is said to have led to a very sharp increase in market research and product change by native Yugoslav soft-drinks concerns.

In general, marketing in all three of these countries is affected, by comparison with the Soviet Union, by three other factors that are worth mentioning. First, all are far more dependent on foreign trade than the USSR. The ratio of visible exports to net material product in Hungary is about 40 per cent, and calculations in terms of Western-style GNP are said to give ratios only slightly below those for Denmark, Finland and Norway.[22] Hungarian trade-dependence is greater than for most East European countries, but for all of them, since they are small countries, actual and optimal foreign trade flows are far larger relative to national product than they are for the USSR. Since the USSR and other Comecon countries do around 30 per cent or more of their foreign trade by value outside Comecon (far more, in the case of Yugoslavia, which in 1970 obtained 60.7 per cent of total imports from EEC and EFTA countries[23]), it follows that trade with non-Comecon countries also looms larger in the smaller East European economies than it does in the Soviet economy. Marketing and advertising of exports in Western countries and of imports in the home economy by Western firms have therefore been more important, have led to marketing being taken more seriously, sooner, and have produced a bigger spillover of Western marketing ideas and techniques into the domestic economy.

Secondly, contact with Western countries is generally greater. There are generally more Western visitors and more visits by nationals to the West per 1,000 population in Eastern Europe than in the Soviet Union. Foreign travel is immeasurably freer for residents in the three countries mainly considered here than for Soviet citizens. Marketing people attend conferences and study in Western Europe. In Yugoslavia there are many marketing people who have lived and worked in Western countries. Some have studied at business schools or worked in Western agencies.

Finally, history. In Eastern Europe some people still of working age started work in a pre-war, pre-communist economy. In the USSR, apart from people from the Baltic states and other areas acquired on the eve of World War Two,

[22] *Hungary Today*, p. 135.
[23] Davy, The Times (25 June 1971) p. 12.

very few people even remember a pre-communist society. For this and perhaps other reasons people in Yugoslavia, Hungary, Czechoslovakia, Poland and East Germany, at least, feel themselves on the whole to be mentally part of the Western world. It is far easier for them to understand Western business methods and Western society generally than it is for Russians. The decline of the censorship in some countries also helps.

In the East European countries that I have not considered in detail here central planning is more detailed and extensive than in Hungary. Broadly speaking, their arrangements are closer to those of the Soviet Union. In Czechoslovakia, reforms somewhat similar to the Hungarian reforms were being introduced before the invasion. Since 1968 the industrial ministries have been re-established and there has been a re-centralisation of economic management. In Bulgaria, Romania and the DDR (East Germany) there have been reforms, but they have generally been of the more limited Soviet kind, together with a development of industrial associations and some devolution of powers to them. The East German industrial assocations initially were financially autonomous groupings, and have aroused considerable interest among some Soviet reformers. The DDR and Bulgaria have also aimed at more sophisticated, rational and (ideally) computable centralised planning methods, as do some Soviet planners and politicians. The tendency in the past two years has been on the whole to re-centralise decision-making, with some loss of 'rights' by enterprises and/or associations to higher bodies. The DDR has more developed and sophisticated marketing organisations than the other 'non-market' socialist countries, but in general the domestic marketing environment is perhaps not very different in any of these countries, allowing for differences in consumption levels, from the Soviet environment.

7 The organisation and functions of advertising

Poland

The formal organisation of Polish advertising closely resembles that of Soviet advertising. This is hardly surprising. In the previous chapter it was argued that the Polish economy is still highly centralised and close to the Soviet model, with a marketing environment fairly similar to the Soviet one. Advertising and marketing have so far had only a limited development, as in the USSR, and chapter 8 shows that total advertising expenditure is still very small.

Like the Russians, the Poles have one major foreign-trade agency, Agpol (corresponding to the Soviet Vneshtorgreklama), and a hierarchical structure in domestic advertising, with a top policy body, the Advertising Planning Council (APC), which in turn corresponds to the Soviet Inter-Departmental Council on Advertising. We will look at the organisation of foreign-trade and domestic advertising in that order.

Agpol does not have a complete monopoly of foreign trade advertising, but its work is entirely in the foreign-trade field: either for Polish goods and services abroad or for exporters to Poland. It is the only Polish advertising organisation that could reasonably be called an agency. That is to say, it is primarily a specialist intermediary between advertisers and media, booking space and time and offering campaign planning advice and creative work. Much of what it does, of course, has the special character of a Comecon foreign trade agency's work. It produces material for the official monthly *Handel Zagraniczny* (*Foreign Trade*); it does no market research, in the usual sense, on Polish markets, though it does conduct desk research on foreign markets; about three-quarters of the promotional work it does in Poland (i.e. for imports) is for industrial producer goods. Its turnover is

dominated by press advertising—especially technical press—
exhibition and technical symposiums, with television
and radio advertising playing only a minor role—press and
exhibition work accounted for about 74 per cent of Agpol
turnover in 1970, and television and radio for only 5 per
cent. Its neon and direct mail turnover (with relatively large
production costs probably included in the former) both
appear to be larger than its radio and television turnover at
present. However, if the very large increase in consumer-goods imports planned for 1971 (28 per cent above
the 1970 level) reflects a real and lasting change in Polish
import priorities, Agpol's media-mix will no doubt change.

In the Polish market much of its work at present is with
main buying influences in ministries, industrial associations
and foreign-trade organisations, and also with specialist
technical journals. In Western markets it has links with
Western agencies and may commission work from them. It is
therefore the main channel by which Western marketing
methods enter the Polish economy. It does not however deal
primarily with Western clients and markets. The bulk of its
work is with Comecon exporters, who account for about
three-quarters of its turnover (which, oddly enough, is rather
higher than their share in Polish foreign-trade turnover).
Apart from its agents abroad, Agpol has a staff of about 150,
nearly all in Warsaw.

There is no comparable organisation in domestic marketing. There are three specialist advertising organisations, all
attached to the internal distributive system: one to the state
retail and wholesale network, one to the urban co-operative
network and one to the rural co-operative network.[1] These
organisations are not at present agencies so much as
producers of advertising equipment and material (neon signs,
shop-window mannequins, printed publicity material, etc.),
with some limited agency functions. The marketing and
distribution with which they are concerned is almost exclusively that of consumer goods. The allocation of producer
goods is done largely by separate organisations and little

[1] As appendix 2 to chapter 5 shows, the co-operative systems account
for about half of total retail turnover.

marketing is involved in it, since administrative allocation prevails.

There are also advertising sections in some consumer-goods enterprises, usually consisting of one, two or three people. The industrial associations in the consumer sector also have advertising sections. The relevant branch ministries have advertising councils, whose chairmen are also members of the top-level co-ordinating body, the APC. These councils are partly gatherings of 'outsiders', including academics, who advise on marketing policies; they also include the handful of ministry staff concerned with advertising. The Ministry of Culture and the media are also represented on the APC. Since enterprises are grouped into associations, and associations are subordinates to ministries, every advertising section and organisation is ultimately subordinate to someone represented on the APC.

This structure is almost identical with the Soviet one except for the Soviet Union's division of consumer-sector ministries (and advertising organisations) between Union ministries in Moscow and their subordinate republic counterparts in the different republics. Like the Soviet formal organisation, it suggests a high degree of central control of advertising but does not seem to exert detailed operational control in practice.

Enterprises, associations and ministries in the consumer sector usually have advertising budgets. Their advertising sections or councils plan various advertising activities (in the broad sense used throughout this paper) on a yearly basis. Plans at association and ministry level include, at least in broad terms, the plans of subordinate units, and at each stage there should be vetting, co-ordination, aggregation and finally approval of subordinate units' intended marketing activities. In general, each unit's spending in each year is within an advertising appropriation approved by a superior body. So, as one would expect in a centralised system, the autonomy of each business unit, in advertising, up to and including ministry level, is circumscribed. It is not usually easy to transfer funds between expenditure heads — at least openly. Enterprises may draw on their association's centralised advertising appropriation in addition to their own, but that is

apparently the main form of financial flexibility. The
enterprises may also, on the other hand, have to contribute
to an association or ministry joint campaign.

It would appear, none the less, that co-ordination and
control from above are mainly concerned with financial
limits. Ministries submit advertising budgets, major campaign
plans and some media and product details to the APC. The
latter has the power to alter budgets in two cases: first, in
pursuit of a government policy which diverges from the
ministries' and associations' plans for marketing particular
products. Thus extra funds may be made available for
advertising products on non-commercial grounds, e.g. tooth-
paste for reasons of health. Similarly there was a cen-
trally-planned policy of marketing margarine domestically at
the expense of butter, to reduce the pressures of (potential)
domestic demand for an important exportable product, on
balance of payments grounds. Second, when particular
advertising plans are considered 'wasteful' or 'unnecessary',
they may be cut.

These powers are not negligible, and it would be difficult
for anyone to launch a campaign of any size without APC
formal approval. However, within advertising appropriation
limits there is some flexibility and scope for initiative at
lower levels, especially in advertising goods classified as
luxuries. Moreover, the APC does not appear systematically
to comb through branch marketing plans and co-ordinate
them in a very sophisticated way with national production
and consumption plans.

There does not, in short, appear to be a national
advertising plan, except in a loose sense. Ministries are said to
prepare their advertising plans without knowing what other
ministries are planning. If, as seems to be the case, APC
consideration of these plans is confined to vetting financial
limits, together with some *ad hoc* intervention on national
policy grounds, it would probably be wrong to think of the
outcome as a sort of national plan for advertising, though
there are elements of adjustment and control from above.

In any case advertising plans, like any plans anywhere,
are not necessarily fulfilled. In one instance quoted to me,
the Ministry of the Food Industry had a 46 million zloty

appropriation for 1970 and spent only 38 million. So whatever co-ordination there is at the national level would appear to be only of an approximate kind. It limits, but does not closely dictate, what actually happens (unless there was a process of continuing fine adjustment from above throughout the year, which I doubt).

Some inter-branch co-ordination occurs at lower levels, however. This may well be more important. The industrial associations are said to plan their advertising in conjunction with the wholesale organisations (under the Ministry of Internal Trade), which buy from them and sell to the retail network. These organisations have data on stocks and retail sales, generated by the Trade Ministry's plan-fulfilment reporting system. This is in effect the main kind of market research used for planning advertising policies (as in the USSR), and perhaps the only kind that is any use (for short-term planning) in an administrative economy with sellers' markets.

So much for formal organisation. Let us now ask a more important question: who advertises what, and why?

Here again, the picture is not very different from that in the Soviet Union. Advertising is carried out mainly by distributors rather than producers.[2] It is said that about one-third of domestic advertising expenditure is incurred by producers and about two-thirds by the internal trade system. There are some joint campaigns, financed equally by trade and industry. It is held by some specialists, at least, that industry does not usually play an active role in formulating advertising policy, but simply contributes some of the finance.

This situation resembles the Soviet one, and seems to be the natural outcome of a combination of a Soviet-type administrative economic system with sellers' markets on the

[2] Advertising is defined here, as usual, in a wide sense to include a good deal of below-the-line promotional spending. Since East European data usually include some shop-window display expenditure they are bound, other things equal, to show a larger share of spending by retailers than advertising data that exclude such point-of-sale promotion. But even if this is excluded on the East European side, the statement in the text remains true.

one hand, and 'middling' Comecon consumption levels on the other. Thus, in Poland, as in the USSR, there is an 'administrative market' between consumer-goods producers and internal trade, and most producers can dispose of their output very easily, without paying much attention to the state of the final demand for it.

This does not mean, however, that the state of final demand is completely unimportant for them. As long as distributors generally find themselves operating in sellers' markets *vis-à-vis* final consumers, they have little incentive to exert much influence on the assortment of goods delivered to them by producers. What is scarce is gratefully accepted; it will also be worth accepting some unwanted and potentially unsaleable (at existing prices) goods in order not to alienate suppliers who are also sources of scarce products. Therefore distributors, encumbered with some surpluses, incur advertising expenditure while producers need not bother.

However, once a substantial number of personal real incomes have risen to levels at which there is significant discretionary buying power, as they have in both the USSR and Poland, the relative importance of 'surplus', or potentially surplus, goods in total supplies to retail outlets increases, the balance of power shifts somewhat from producers to distributors, and the readiness of the trade network to reject unwanted supplies, i.e. to resist administrative allocation, increases. There then arise more and more cases where producers have trouble in disposing of products and resort to product changes and/or advertising and promotion to meet their output, sales or profit targets. This process, as the previous chapter pointed out, seems to have gone further in Poland than in the USSR,[3] and can only be expected to go further still in both countries.

In this situation product innovation in the consumer sector becomes more active, and this in turn creates a further demand for advertising. It is said that the advertising of new products in Poland is carried out mainly by industry rather than trade, with the latter concentrating on surplus, or

[3] The relative lack of queues in Warsaw shops, compared with Moscow, is probably an indication of this. Private production and trade may have been important in plugging gaps in supply and offering competition.

potentially surplus, established product lines. If this is so, it suggests that Polish industry may be a bit more aware of the uses of marketing than Soviet industry.[4] Given the closer links that Polish society has with the outside world, and the greater importance of foreign trade (including trade with the West) in the Polish economy, this would not be surprising. However, there have been cases, as in the USSR, where industry has refused to contribute to campaigns for some of its products.

The very broad product-group mix of Polish advertising, described in chapter 8 below, fits in with this overall picture. The large share of advertising taken by non-food goods relative to food (and probably by consumer durables, within the former group) probably reflects both relative degrees of scarcity at existing prices and relative rates of product innovation, though to demonstrate this quantitatively would require much more data than are available.

As for the process of advertising, it appears that enterprise and association advertising sections typically decide what and how to advertise on their own initiative (within their appropriations and sometimes with some instructions from above), and do their own media booking, exhibition organising or ordering of printed promotional matter, etc. The media of course will increase their revenue by taking on more advertising, but much of this additional revenue is paid out to the artists and designers (often freelance) who do the creative work. It is not clear that the media management generally have a strong financial inducement to accept advertising, since their revenues are in any case underwritten by the state with actual or potential subsidies, there are strong influences 'from above' on the amount and nature of editorial matter and total space and time are also limited by decisions 'from above' and shortages (e.g. of newsprint).

A certain technical backwardness also affects the pattern of advertising; e.g. in colour photography and quality of

---

[4] A common sequence of events in the USSR was for a new product to be produced and distributed without any marketing expenditure by the producer. Retail sales problems then forced distributors either to stop ordering from industry or to advertise themselves to make the product known. See chapter 4 ('Product-mix') above.

paper, though Polish graphic work, for example, can be very good. All these constraints on advertising are reminiscent of Soviet marketing, though they may be less severe. It is probable that the number of display advertisements encountered by the average Polish citizen per day, though well below West European levels, is higher than in the USSR, partly because of the greater relative importance of marketing by Western exporters but mainly because domestic marketing is rather more developed. The average total daily radio advertising time is said to be one hour twenty minutes, in five or six commercial spots. Television advertising is less, but is said to be increasing fast.[5]

What influence does state policy have on the content of advertising? The kinds of top-level intervention that can occur in the allocation of advertising expenditure between products have already been described. On social grounds such as health policy, or on grounds of economic policy such as the maintenance of supplies for export or the containing of inflationary pressure, top policy-makers may require some product lines to be especially promoted and others to be especially played down. There was also some reference, in interviews, to consumption 'norms' or (roughly) long-term per capita consumption targets in physical terms.[6] These however do not seem to figure so prominently in Polish as in Soviet consumption planning.

Similarly, there are severe limits on the extent to which sex and status appeal can be used in Polish advertising, and an official preference for 'informative' over 'persuasive' advertising, of course, exists. As in the Soviet Union, however, it is hard to separate the effects of official social control from the naïveté to be expected of advertising in its earliest and most innocent stage of development. In any case, serious and intelligent discussion of social questions is normal in Poland but abnormal in the USSR, and Polish specialists neither oversimplify these issues nor put great emphasis upon them, as Russian specialists do (at least in articles and in interviews with foreigners).

[5] Agpol, *Rate and Data* (Warsaw, n.d.) p. 2.
[6] See the appendix to chapter 4 for a description of Soviet consumption 'norms'.

Future developments in Polish advertising will depend crucially on the extent and nature of changes in the economic system. Under the present, broadly Soviet-type, centralized organisation of economic management advertising will no doubt continue to develop, but only in a limited way. As incomes and per capita physical supplies increase a greater proportion of consumer spending tends to acquire a discretionary nature and sellers' markets in consumer goods ease, provided that total disposable money incomes are not allowed to rise much faster than total supplies at existing prices, intensifying repressed inflationary pressures. This development stimulates marketing and advertising activities, and they might reasonably be expected to increase in importance — relative to, say, total consumer spending. The revised five-year plan directives of the post-Gomulka leadership put greater stress than before on raising the output of consumer goods and services. If this actually happens the process will be strengthened.

It is hard to envisage a dramatic change in the position of advertising, however, unless there is a radical de-centralisation of economic management, with producers operating as substantially autonomous, profit-seeking units, with market relationships with the distributive system. Only then would most producers face competition and become market-oriented. Marketing expenditure would then shift substantially from trade to industry and from below-the-line promotion to media advertising, and domestic agencies would develop, working as specialist intermediaries and not closely controlled by either trade or industrial units. The raising of consumption levels makes such de-centralisation more likely. This is because it increases discretionary purchasing power and makes centralised control of consumer-goods output and centralised allocation to distributors more and more difficult to maintain without making people increasingly irritable at not getting exactly what they want and at being offered what they don't (exactly) want.

Hungary
With Hungarian advertising, we come to our first case of advertising in a market-oriented socialist economy. The

organisational differences are at once apparent. It must be remembered, however, that the New Economic Mechanism dates only from the beginning of 1968 and that, despite all the careful preparation and the very brisk and wholesale introduction of the reforms, the system is still in a trial-and-error state. Marketing is still adapting to new circumstances and will no doubt have to adapt to further changes, which will not necessarily be in the direction of further de-centralisation.

It must also be remembered that some of the equipment and marketing ideas now in use date from an earlier period and that Budapest in particular has been a sophisticated modern city much longer than it has been a socialist capital. The numerous Parisian-style advertising rotundas on the pavements, now well covered with commercial posters, date from before World War Two. Transport and press advertising seems to have survived to some extent through the post-war period, with classified ads (including marriage ads) quite numerous from 1956 on.

At all events, Budapest now bristles with advertisements. No doubt the immediate impression that a foreign visitor gets is misleading, because the density of street and transport posters and neon advertising is closer to West European levels than are the levels of commercial time on radio and television or of press advertising space, and these latter forms of advertising are not immediately perceptible. No doubt a count would show that the average number of commercial messages that an inhabitant of Budapest encounters per day is well below West European levels. None the less, the amount of advertising going on is manifestly higher than in Poland or the USSR, and the role of advertising is clearly more 'Western'.

The organisation of advertising reflects these differences. There are generally agreed to be two major organisations that could be regarded as agencies — the Hungexpo Advertising Agency and Magyar Hirdeto. Before the 1968 reforms they were cast in the standard Comecon mould in that they had monopolies of, and were confined to, foreign and home trade respectively. Since 1968, their statutory monopolies have (at their own urging as well as by the overall logic of the reforms), been revoked, and they compete in both home and foreign markets. They remain subordinate, in the last resort, to the Ministries of Foreign and Internal Trade, and their clients and spheres of operation naturally still reflect their pre-1968 roles to a considerable extent. The Hungexpo agency still works mainly in foreign-trade advertising; both the agency and the Budapest International Fair are divisions of the Hungexpo organisation which is subordinate to the Ministry of Foreign Trade. Magyar Hirdeto is still dominant in domestic media advertising, especially press, poster and neon.

These two major organisations also provide agency services, including creative work. However, they retain a direct ownership of or contractual relationship with certain media. Thus Magyar Hirdeto has an exclusive contract, still operating, which gives it almost all Budapest transport advertising. It also owns some poster sites, neon signs and pavement rotundas and has very strong links with certain newspapers.[7]

It is probably desirable, in the long run, that both organisations should become completely specialised and unattached intermediaries, completely credible as objective advisers on media selection.

In the meantime they are large organisations (Magyar Hirdeto has a staff of 500 in Budapest and 250 in the provinces) with a wide range of activities. Magyar Hirdeto has a large press-clipping service, and claims to be the first agency in the world to offer a radio and television monitoring service to commercial subscribers.

There is also the fair-sized (150 staff) and, from the evidence available to me, very professional Orszagos Piackutato Intezet (Hungarian Institute of Market Research), which provides desk and field research (currently about 70—100 studies a year), opinion surveys, some advertising

---

[7] Magyar Hirdeto's history is remarkably varied. This no doubt helps to account for its apparently fairly long established *de facto* independence and wide range of activities. It was founded in 1948 from three media advertising departments (including one film and one radio). At first it was subordinate to the Ministry of Transport, then to the Ministry of Internal Trade. From 1952 to 1960 it was under the Ministry of Culture and from 1960 again under the Ministry of Internal Trade.

effectiveness research (also carried out by Magyar Hirdeto), the product-supply information bulletins mentioned in the previous section, a design/quality-mark centre and marketing periodicals, and has recently gone into the exhibition and show-room business.

These three organisations are self-financing, profit-seeking units with a high degree of autonomy. They are not budget-financed. They operate within a framework of state regulations, and might in special circumstances be subject to direct instructions 'from above', but for practical purposes they are autonomous business units. They seek and accept business, hire and fire, obtain credit and diversify on their own initiative, like most production and distribution units under the New Economic Mechanism. They are different in nature from any enterprises or organisations in a Soviet-type economy. On the other hand, the ministries, and ultimately the government, have reserve powers to disband or amal-gamate them, or to limit their sphere of action, as with any Hungarian enterprise. They are therefore not part of a state management hierarchy, on the one hand, but on the other hand they lack some of the sovereignty of a Western private firm.

In a small economy the two major agencies have a strong position. More competition would probably be healthier. Under the New Economic Mechanism it is possible to form new co-operative enterprises fairly freely, and some small 'advertising' firms have sprung up. They are however not generally agencies but specialists in printing, photographic or graphic work, etc. Also, some of the media have expanded their advertising sections, which may be active in seeking out customers. But agency competition reduces to Magyar Hirdeto versus Hungexpo.

So far as national policy and control is concerned, there is no mechanism for centralised financial control of advertising, nor is there any machinery for co-ordination and national planning in this field. The planning machinery and financial rules and price controls, as described in the previous chapter, guide enterprises towards a high rate of investment, help to mould the pattern of investment and regulate the balance of payments, thus setting certain very broad limits to the advertising that enterprises will be able and willing to finance. The same might be said of any Western country, perhaps, but there are two differences. One is that the remaining price controls almost certainly make it harder, generally, to recoup heavy advertising expenditure by deliberate pricing policy. The other difference concerns informal government influence.

The following example may bring out the sort of government suasion that can affect a firm's marketing policy. It should however be noted that there is some disagreement among Hungarian advertising people I spoke to about the significance of this example, and indeed about what precisely happened. One version, at all events, was as follows. The market for coffee is competitive and relatively well supplied. Heavy (by Hungarian standards) competitive advertising developed. It is claimed that state planners, by arguing that substantially increased imports were not going to be allowed in the near future so that there was little prospect of a general growth in sales, persuaded the main combatants to cut advertising expenditure in their own interests. A somewhat similar case history is claimed for detergents. A sort of Johnsonian reasoning together or French *economie concertée*, all velvet glove and no iron hand, is claimed to have done the trick. If so, there must have been some sort of multilateral disarmament agreement among competitors. If really ravenous competition were to develop in some sector, purely voluntary planning might have difficulty in containing it.[8]

The function of advertising, then, is in principle very close to its function in Western economies: to promote the sales of independent, profit-maximising business units. This is perhaps moderated by greater scope for informal government suasion, whose strength derives partly from mental habits learned in the old system and partly from the fairly strong planning systems and the reserve powers of the authorities.

The difference from Poland and the USSR is considerable. For a start, producers tend to have more incentive to

[8] The experience of French planners with the motor industry comes to mind.

advertise in Hungary and distributors (relatively) less. In 1970 the share of distribution in Magyar Hirdeto's turnover was as low as 19 per cent. In total national advertising it is higher; one estimate puts the distributive sector's share of total advertising expenditure (in the broad sense used here) at about half. But this should be compared to a two-thirds share in Poland. Moreover, the difference in incentives to advertise between the two countries is larger than the figures suggest because the Poles, like the Russians, to some extent *require* industry to share the burden of advertising expenditure with the trade system, willy nilly. In Hungary advertisers advertise to whatever extent they themselves consider desirable. If Polish expenditure were equally voluntary, the producers' share would be less than a third and the trade share higher than two-thirds.

The effects of the new Hungarian system should also show up in a more 'Western' media and product mix. Detailed media and product breakdowns are unfortunately not available, however, for both Poland and Hungary, so comparison here is impossible. None the less, the fragmentary data collected in chapter 8 seem to support what one would expect *a priori* about the media mix, namely, that at least some of the above-the-line media are relatively more important in Hungary, especially press and outdoor advertising.

I would also expect Hungarian advertising to be spread over a wider range of goods and service, since buyers' markets are more widespread than in Poland and the USSR. Casual observation of television, press and poster advertising tends to support this view, but there are no systematic data. Most groups of consumer products seem to be advertised on one or more of these media — many foods and beverages, minor household items (from detergents to bathroom fittings), consumer durables and services. Branding is prominent and there are certainly markets (such as coffee and detergents, mentioned above) where brand competition has been fairly strong. To a Western visitor, of course, Western brands (AGIP, Pepsi, Chanel and many others) are especially conspicuous, but they certainly do not predominate.

So far as advertising other than consumer-goods display advertising is concerned, it is clear that classified advertising is vastly more developed than in Poland or the USSR. Several Budapest papers carry pages of small advertisements every day. The extent to which industrial marketing has developed is less clear. One view is that, if data were available, they would show that Hungarian enterprises are spending a substantial amount on below-the-line, promotional activities for producer goods. Other specialists consider that industrial marketing is so far relatively less developed than consumer-goods marketing because there is still a strong tendency to sellers' markets for most producer goods. Western firms trying to break into the Hungarian market, of course, are active in this field, mainly in exhibitions, technical symposia, printed promotional matter and technical press advertising.

In general the Hungarians, having chosen a competitive market-socialist economic system, seem to regard competitive advertising as a natural corollary of such a sytem. This does not mean that their advertising will necessarily develop 'capitalist' proportions and entirely 'capitalist' characteristics. This point will be taken up in the conclusions. For the meantime, we can note three things. First, an advertising code has yet to be adopted. One was worked out and published recently, for discussion purposes. It is generally close to that of the International Chamber of Commerce. A voluntary self-imposed code is likely to be agreed. Other controls seem also to be rather non-ideological. As was mentioned earlier, a pre-communist 1920s law on the regulation of business competition has been invoked under the New Economic Mechanism in cases where unfair competition is claimed. It is not yet clear whether, for example, there will be any law, voluntary code or informal agreement over knocking copy. It is clear that criticism of a rival's product is actionable if it is factually untrue; it is not clear that there will be any restraint of any kind on knocking copy that is also fair comment. The fact that issues like this are real in Hungary is some indication of how competitive marketing is becoming.

Second, advertising is not subjected to a censorship apparatus. But press editors, for example, exercise self-censorship, judging what is acceptable and what is not. A

Western advertisement which used a 'Best People Drink Brand-X Whisky' line was refused by some editors but accepted by others, with no political repercussions. One would expect both sex and status to be used relatively lightly in advertising messages, but the limits are not clear.

Finally, attitudes to the uses of advertising seem to be pragmatic. Medium-run (five years or so) plans for the development of advertising seem to be entirely in the nature of forecasts. A doubling in expenditure by 1975 is envisaged, with specially rapid increases in the advertising of prepared foods, light clothing, do-it-yourself items and cosmetics and materials and equipment for housework. These forecasts are based on national and sectoral development plans, but such plans (as in West European indicative planning) are not binding on business units. The fairly strong controls that policy-makers have over the pattern of investment and hence the broad sectoral structure of the economy should have the side-effect of setting the product-group structure of advertising, but only in the very broadest terms and not by any direct control. Within these broad sectoral development plans there should be scope for marketing activities themselves to affect the product mix by influencing demand — to whatever extent the mysterious power of advertising actually does affect demand.

State policy seems likely to influence advertising more directly in some areas. For example, with the proposed rapid expansion of car ownership (60—65 per cent more cars on the road by 1975), a large road-safety campaign is planned. This sort of thing has its obvious counterparts in the West. A more Eastern kind of state 'steering' of advertising is represented by plans to lighten the rich Hungarian diet on health grounds, partly by advertising directed by the Ministry of Internal Trade. If Hungarians persist in preferring a short, plump, happy life of dumplings and paprika sauce, however, it would seem to be in the spirit of the new Hungarian system for the authorities to give in to them. Finally, total press space and radio and television time seem to be under fairly direct central control. I doubt whether the authorities would permit a situation in which these media were dominated (quantitatively) by advertising. This could be an important constraint on advertising expenditure on these media. How much such a constraint would also limit total advertising expenditure would depend on mainly economic considerations.

Yugoslavia

For the reasons given in chapter 6, one would expect advertising to be further developed in Yugoslavia than in Hungary. The quantitative evidence in chapter 8, though very uncertain and unreliable, tends to support this prediction. The picture that one obtains of advertising organisation also seems to support it.

However, the Socialist Federal Republic of Yugoslavia is harder to generalise about than most small countries, and much of what will be said here refers to the more developed parts of the country and especially to Croatia. The uneven, and in some regions low, level of economic development make marketing conditions in Yugoslavia unusually varied. Hungary, though a more recent exemplar of market social-ism, is also a country with higher average living standards and with very small regional income variations. So despite what has been said in the previous paragraph, one might well feel a lot farther from a mass-consumption society in, say, Mace-donia than by Lake Balaton. Consumer-goods producers, and some manufacturers of producer goods, do extensive advert-ising and tend to have their own advertising sections. Specialist marketing organisations are profit-sharing workers' self-management concerns, like other enterprises, not subord-inate to ministries. State and party control over them, as over Yugoslav enterprises generally, is restricted to the net-revenue distribution rules and other indirect controls mentioned in the previous chapter.

The formal autonomy of these organisations has tended to grow. Until recently the regional authorities had a fifty per cent voting share in the appointment of directors of enterprises; this has now been surrendered entirely to the workers' councils. So the most strikingly socialist feature of Yugoslav agencies and market research organisations is that ultimate control is vested in the employees. (Private firms are not important in this field.) These agencies are not directed 'from above'. They seek profits in what is in principle a competitive, guided-market environment.

It is generally agreed that marketing and advertising were little developed until quite recently. The market environment has been gradually evolved in a series of reforms, with the last major one in 1965. The opening of the economy to Western trade and, more recently, investment has also been a gradual process, and this also has exerted a growing influence on the marketing situation. (Commercial advertising is said, however, to have developed initially out of purely domestic competition and particular surpluses of goods.) Therefore most specialist marketing concerns are young and, so far as their sphere of activity and internal structure are concerned, still evolving.

There are said to be three hundred registered advertising organisations. One view is that several, perhaps five or six, could be described as full-service agencies. But perhaps only one of these, the Zagreb agency OZEHA, is a substantial, full-service agency without media attachments. It has five branch offices and a staff of two hundred. The newspapers *Vjesnik*, *Politika* and *Borba* and some television stations have developed their own specialist advertising agencies. Like Magyar Hirdeto in Budapest, though probably to a greater extent, their media links preclude them from being 'pure' (for want of a better word) agencies. There are about ten firms offering marketing consultancy of various kinds, and the rest of the three hundred are specialist organisations doing photographic work, exhibitions, printing, etc. There is no statutory home-trade — foreign-trade distinctions between agencies. In addition to advertising organisations there is a major market research organisation, ZIT, which operates on a federal scale with a staff of about a hundred and does market research for some of the agencies as well as for domestic producers and foreign firms.

Organisation is extremely flexible and decentralised. At present a great deal of advertising does not go through agencies, but as they further develop their share will no doubt rise. Agencies operate on a mixture of 15 per cent commissions and service fees. For small accounts, fees are usual. OZEHA also has some partnership schemes with major clients, in which it supplies a complete market-planning service and receives a percentage of profits. It also has open-books agreements (access to each other's accounts) with its full-service clients.

Apparently there would be no formal difficulty in setting up a new agency. It would not be possible to set up a private business of sufficient size to operate as more than a very small creative boutique, but workers' self-management agency could, as was mentioned earlier, be founded on the initiative of a few people. The economic barriers to successful market entry, however, are substantial. It is difficult to compete with strong media-linked agencies likely to be favoured by their own media, possibly by hidden rebates. And since much of the market for marketing is limited to a republic, rather than the country as a whole, it is hard to displace an existing large agency from markets which it already dominates.

Technically, Yugoslav marketing is probably ahead of that of any of the Comecon countries. One indication of this is the extent to which major Western firms with great expertise in marketing will now use Yugoslav agency and market research services. Firms with licencing agreements enabling their branded products to be made in Yugoslavia can plan their marketing in detail from abroad. They can also use Western agencies. Yet in several cases they make substantial use of Yugoslav agencies — e.g. Pepsi — OZEHA.

OZEHA has its own television and photographic studio and a creative department headed by a Yugoslav former 'economic emigrant' with considerable experience of creative work in Western agencies. Unlike most East European agencies, it relies mainly on its own staff for art work, and not on freelance artists. Its larger accounts are of the order of 10 million new dinars (£4¼m.) a year, and it seems to be active in all main media. At present 70 per cent of its turnover is in media work rather than below-the-line promotional work (exhibitions, fairs, etc.). This is high for an East European agency, and is expected to rise.

Yugoslav advertising in general is closer to a West European media and product mix than is advertising in any Comecon country. The data on this in chapter 8 are not reliable. However, they probably have too narrow a coverage and understate both the totals and some components, and therefore at least do not overstate the importance of the less-used media and less-advertised product groups. One indication of the increasing variety of media used is that direct mail has been developed to some extent. Another is that television advertising had developed beyond the few, scattered and undifferentiated blocks of advertising time typical in Comecon countries, to some segmentation of commercial time and adaptation to particular audiences. As was mentioned earlier, there is now a proposal for a second channel with 100 per cent commercial sponsorship. Fashion magazines are as decadent as the best. A very wide range of goods and services are advertised, as the data in chapter 8 suggest. Advertising of machinery and other producer goods in specialist periodicals is quite developed, and most of the kinds of consumer goods that are advertised in Britain seem to be advertised in Yugoslavia as well. The data in chapter 8 also show (without much doubt) that the share of distributors in spending on advertising and promotion is relatively small — a market-economy trait — and smaller than in Hungary. Much of what is classified as distributors' spending in Yugoslavia, moreover, is by importers rather than retailers.

The Yugoslav marketing environment has in recent years had one important market-economy characteristic that clearly distinguished it from that of a Soviet-type economy and even from that of post-1967 Hungary: substantial retail price rises. Compared with a typically Soviet-type situation in which (recently) costs rise but retail prices do not, this open inflation has probably tended to assist the development of marketing. To begin with, it means that margins of price over production and distribution costs are not fixed or squeezed for long periods, so that it is probably easier than in a fixed-price situation to adjust them deliberately in order to finance increased selling costs.[9] Secondly, it is of course the alternative to shortages and sellers' markets under conditions

---

[9] In situations of open inflation the rise in producers' selling prices may lag behind the rise in their costs, but the reverse is often, and may well be more usually, the case.

of inflationary pressure. Where prices can and do rise in conditions of excess aggregate demand, individual markets are more likely to be in equilibrium at any point of time than if inflation is repressed. In such markets there is far more incentive to advertise than in sellers' markets. It is also true, admittedly, that the situation allows more scope for relative price changes as between pairs of competing products, so that price competition may be used instead of non-price (advertising) competition. Still the comparison is with markets in which competition of any kind is weak, so that this is just a minor offsetting factor so far as the development of advertising is concerned.

After all that has been said about the Yugoslav marketing situation, one might ask whether it differs qualitatively in any important respect from that in, say, Britain. I put this question myself in interviews, and the following would appear to be the answer.[10] There are felt to be three main differences from a West European environment. First, there is less competition in many markets, partly because of surviving (and recently re-introduced) price controls. Second, there are fewer experienced marketing people, less specialisation (e.g. in commercial printing, photography, artwork, etc.) and a lower technical level. Some services such as specialised typography cannot be obtained locally at all. Television commercials have tended to be made by regular television studio staff who are not specialists in commercials (this is why OZEHA set up their own television studio).[11] Thirdly, the workers' self-management system makes it harder to sack people. In general, it is an egalitarian system, which some people would expect to blunt entrepreneurial incentives and others would not. There are few capital gains, and even fewer that can be legally kept to a small group of people. Directors cannot award themselves very large salaries, since they have the workers' council breathing down their necks. As with

[10] Mr Mihovil Skobe, executive vice-president of OZEHA, suggested these three points and other interviews also tended to produce them.
[11] The (Zagreb) television 'Propagandni Intermezzos' that I saw were sophisticated and well made, but practitioners say that commercial effectiveness tends to lose out to art for art's sake — a phenomenon not peculiar to socialist countries.

British tax rates, there is no good evidence at all, one way or the other, about the effects of these egalitarian constraints on performance.

Direct state intervention in marketing activities is clearly thought of as rare, though price controls and intervention in foreign trade decisions are held to make the marketing environment less stable than it would be for most Western firms. As in Hungary, an advertising code has been proposed. It, too, is closely based on the International Code.[12] It is proposed that violence and pornography should be avoided. Interpretation and practice might be a bit more austere than in Britain, but differences are not obvious. Advertisements may not attack the system of workers' self-management. This would be the Yugoslav equivalent of blasphemy, and probably not much of a selling point anyway.[13]

[12] See the article by Dr F. Rocco in the journal of the Yugoslav Marketing Association, *Marketing*, no. 1 (Zagreb, 1971).
[13] In the aftermath of the troubles of late 1971, which were triggered off by the issue of budgetary allocations between the constituent republics of Yugoslavia, but which also raised broader issues of central federal control over the different national groups and the extent of social liberalisation and Western influence in some areas, there was some curtailment of the more ostentatious display of decadent Western influence — public sale of girlie magazines, for example. This may possibly have led to stronger state control of the content of advertisements since the above was written.

8 Advertising expenditure data

Statistics on advertising expenditure in Eastern Europe, as in many countries, are neither extensive, detailed nor reliable. This chapter gives the figures available for Poland, Hungary and Yugoslavia. It seems that large-scale surveys, such as the one conducted by the Advertising Association for the UK, would be needed to improve on these data. No such survey exists so far, though in Yugoslavia ZIT is beginning something equivalent.

The questions for which I have tried to get numerical answers can be seen in appendix B, at the end of this book. For each country considered in detail here I tried to assemble statistics of total advertising expenditure in the most recent year for which they were available, the rates of growth of that expenditure over a recent period; the composition of expenditure by media and product groups and by the categories of classified, consumer-goods and producer-goods advertising. I also tried to get the more important problems of definition sorted out and to get specialists' judgements on the reliability of the figures. The definition of total advertising expenditure for which data are available varies between these countries, but in each case it is wide, and includes most of what we would call 'below-the-line' or 'promotion' expenditure as well as media advertising.[1]

In general, the result was that rough aggregate data for several recent years were available, though of varying reliability, but data on the composition of expenditure were not. From partial information, however, some broad judgements about composition are possible. One general point

[1] See appendix B for the maximum coverage considered and, B for a discussion of the concepts, Ken Wilmshurst, 'Above or Below? Where to Draw the Line', *Advertising Quarterly* (Spring 1970) pp. 13—19.

about the figures is interesting. The more decentralised the economy, the fewer data were available. In the Soviet-type centralised economy business units are closely monitored and must report their expenditure frequently and in detail to higher authorities. Thus in the case of advertising and marketing expenditure Poland, like the USSR, has a formal supreme co-ordinating body which receives advertising plans and fulfilment reports. These data are not necessarily very good. Some advertising and promotion may not be included, and the cost accounting behind the figures may give a very misleading impression of costs from an economist's point of view.[2] Definitions often are neither clear nor uniform. However, with some adjustments such data give probable orders of magnitude, and the fact that officials in Poland and the USSR told me what they were and were kind enough to spend time discussing them has been a great help.

In Hungary and Yugoslavia, however, the economic system does not automatically generate such data. If you decentralise, you lose some information on aggregates. Special surveys are needed, as in Western countries, to assemble this information again. As enterprises become independent and begin to compete with one another, moreover, the veil of commercial secrecy falls. It may even be difficult to assemble data by special surveys for this reason — as indeed has proved to be the case in Yugoslavia.[3] So these two countries are at a stage where they have lost centralised data and have not yet got round to gathering it by special surveys.

The figures obtained for each country require a good deal of commentary, so they are discussed for each country in turn before any comparisons are made. Where no source is given the data and definitions are from interviews.

---

[2] For example, the costs of enterprise, association or ministry staff and overheads partly accountable to advertising and partly to other activities may not be allocated to advertising at all. Prices used for some services and products entering into advertising costs may not even approximate 'scarcity' prices.

[3] ZIT staff believe that the media generally do not have usable data on their advertising receipts and that enterprises either do not have much data or may be reluctant to supply it. Hence direct estimation, from a census or sample of media *plus* known rates, is believed to be the only way of estimating total media advertising expenditure with any reliability.

Poland

The totals reported by the Ministry of Internal Trade for domestic advertising expenditure are given in table 8.1. These are figures reported to the Advertising Planning Council from below. They have come from shops and enterprises to the associations, and then to the ministries and then to the Council. The 1968 to 1970 inclusive actual expenditure returns are the result of planning, co-ordination and control from above as well as initiative from below.

TABLE 8.1   Polish domestically-financed advertising, 1968—71 plan (m. zlotys).

year	total	percentage increase over previous year
1968	850	—
1969	1100	29.4
1970	1300	18.2
1971 plan	1500	15.4

These figures have the following coverage: media advertising (press, radio, television, cinema, neon, poster, transport) *plus* printed matter (catalogues, leaflets, brochures), exhibitions, free gifts and samples. In addition, some packaging, some shop-window display (probably only for larger stores, which have a separately accounted shop-display section of staff and/or which buy in display work from outside organisations), and some production costs for advertising material to be used abroad. It may also be that marketing expenditure for producer goods (e.g. catalogues, brochures) is under-reported since the data are collected and used primarily for the planning of consumer-goods production and distribution.

The coverage creates some difficulty for comparison because it includes some but not all classes of below-the-line spending. This is probably less important than the doubts about its accuracy. Nobody claims that these figures are very reliable. Apparently some other kinds of spending may be included by reporting enterprises under the heading of advertising. The reporting of advertising expenditure does not follow a unified procedure. The data apparently must be culled from different headings for different kinds of organisation (which gives some idea of the low priority still attached to it). The lowest estimate I was given was that the true figures should be slightly over half of those reported.

One category of advertising in Poland that is excluded from these figures is advertising by foreign firms and organisations. This was put at $1m. in 1970, apparently including expenditure by other socialist countries, whose share was said to be about 74 per cent of the total. Converted into zlotys at the official rates, this suggests that for 1970 a range of probable figures for total advertising expenditure, on the official Polish definition, would be 700m. to 1600m. zlotys. These two figures are the lowest plausible domestic and foreign trade figures combined and the highest plausible domestic and foreign trade figures combined, assuming that the official figures for domestic expenditure are very unlikely indeed to be an under-estimate.

What do these figures mean? Before we do anything pretentious, like comparing them (as a percentage of household expenditure) with other countries' advertsing expenditure, we must bear in mind the snags. First, they do not have exactly the same coverage as other countries' data. This is a common problem. We can however get broadly comparable figures for other countries. Second, costing in Eastern Europe (and the USSR) can be significantly different from general practice in other countries. In particular, overheads and some staff costs are more likely to be included under headings other than advertising where advertising work is relatively unspecialised and agency-like intermediaries handle less of the business. Prices generally are poorer measures of the relative scarcity of resources.

Thirdly, the expenditure level does not reflect so closely the spontaneous willingness of advertisers to undertake advertising and promotion expenditure. Sometimes it is constrained by limits 'from above'. Sometimes it is rather forced on advertisers by central authorities, as when they are required to show fulfilment of a cost plan that includes advertising headings and in which re-shuffling between expenditure heads is not allowed, or when a centralised 'social policy' campaign is organised (such as the recent campaign for margarine as against butter in Poland).

Are the annual rates of growth in the table likely to be about right? If the error each year was of the same relative size and in the same direction, they would be. But since there is simply a large margin of error for each year's figures. and only four years' actual spending is given, we can only conclude that Polish advertising expenditure *seems* to have been growing at something of the order of 20 per cent p.a. This happens to be the same conclusion as for the USSR. As in chapter 3, I conclude that the picture is one of quite rapid growth from extremely low levels of advertising expenditure, but not of the explosive growth to be expected from a radical de-centralisation of the economic system.

On media breakdowns, systematic data are lacking. Table 8.2 summarises the data given to me.

TABLE 8.2   Breakdown of Polish domestic advertising expenditure by media (per cent)

	total domestic advertising 1971 plan	foreign advertising 1969	foreign advertising 1970
press	8.7	44	39
radio & tv	4.7	} 10	5
other			9
neon	} 86.6		
exhibitions		16	12
		30	35

Administrative and production costs are not treated separately but included under the separate media headings. From this very limited information, it is at least clear that what we are calling here 'advertising' expenditure is predominantly below-the-line, non-media spending. Exhibitions and leaflets, brochures and catalogues are almost certainly the largest part of it, as they are in the USSR.

According to the Ministry of Internal Trade the current breakdown of domestic advertising expenditure by major product groups is roughly as shown in table 8.3.

Of advertising in Poland by foreign countries, the general view was that producer goods accounted for about three-quarters of the total. The general picture, then, is probably fairly close to the Soviet one. Foreign trade and domestic

TABLE 8.3   Approximate breakdown of Polish domestic advertising
             expenditure by product group, c.1970 (per cent)

consumer goods and services, of which	95—100
food	25—20
manufactured consumer goods	60—68
services	10—12
producer goods	5—0

advertising differ sharply in product breakdown for two
reasons. First, imports are heavily concentrated on producer
goods. Second, advertising by foreign suppliers to affect
major buying influences in enterprises, combines and industrial ministries (who may seek import allocations from the
Ministry of Foreign Trade if suitably influenced)can be useful.
(This of course includes a great deal of Western firms' staple exhibition and symposium-cum-cocktail-party spending, which is
often the most effective way of getting into an East
European market.) The domestic market in producer goods,
on the other hand, is dominated by centralised allocation,
which usually makes marketing activities redundant. It may
also be, however, that domestic expenditure on what we
would call industrial marketing is under-reported (see above)
— it may be a shade less negligible than it appears.

The large relative size of non-food consumer-goods advertising is interesting. Durables are said to bulk large within this
category, as they do in the USSR. These are typically the
product group where, with rising real incomes but also a
greater ability to expand supply, some surpluses have tended
to emerge in Soviet-type economies.[4] Product innovation is
also commoner in this group than in food products in
Soviet-type economies. Agricultural problems and food shortages have been chronic in the Soviet Union.[5] They have
recently been less important in Poland, but there seems in
some food products to be a government policy of promoting
important food exports in preference to domestic supplies,
and hence of playing down domestic food advertising.

[4] See the Introduction and chapter 4, the first section.
[5] There have been substantial improvements in Soviet agriculture since
the mid-1960s but the very large grain imports of 1972 indicate the
difficulties that still impede rapid, major improvements in Soviet
domestic food supplies.

Hungary

For Hungary, as was explained above, the centralised information of a Soviet-type economy is lacking so far as marketing expenditure is concerned. There have been preliminary attempts to obtain media advertising expenditure totals by sample survey, but at present nobody claims to have good, comprehensive information on it.[6] What we have are estimates with certain known defects for media spending, and guesstimates for below-the-line promotional spending.

The two estimates I obtained have the merit of coming from different sources and of being obtained in different ways.[7] For this reason it is remarkable that they have the further merit of being quite close to one another. I conclude, tentatively, that they are not too far from the truth, though neither their authors nor I would bet heavily on it. For 1969 they are: estimate A, 1,000m. forints; estimate B, 1,200m. forints.

The coverage in each case is narrower than the Polish (and Soviet) figures in that all packaging is apparently excluded. What is included is media *plus* exhibitions, printed promotional matter and some shop-window display.[8] Advertising in Hungary by foreign concerns is included in principle. Classified press advertising is also included.

The growth of advertising expenditure is less clear. Table 8.4 gives some figures.

It is not clear from these figures whether growth in advertising expenditure since the introduction of the New Economic Mechanism has been faster than in Poland and the Soviet Union over the same period. In general, I would expect substantial devolution of decision-making and the introduction of market relationships on the scale of the Hungarian reforms to lead to an explosive growth of advertising expenditure, of the order of 30 per cent or more

[6] Dr Anna Sandor got a less than 50 per cent response rate to a sample survey of 300 enterprises, and considers the respondents to be a substantially unrepresentative sample from a sample that was originally well constructed. Dr Karoly Ravasz has obtained data from media only.
[7] Estimate A is from Dr Ravasz; the other I have derived myself from information on agency turnover and agency executives' opinions about their shares in total advertising expenditure.
[8] By larger stores with separately-accounted display costs.

TABLE 8.4   Hungarian advertising expenditure, various categories, 1967—70

	1967	1968	1969	1st half of 1970	1970
(1) estimate A, media only (m. forints)	98.3*	196.7	261.4	134.2	n.a.
(2) (1) index	100	200	266	137	
(3) estimate B, all forms of advertising (m. forints)	n.a.	n.a.	1200		1500
(4) (3), index			100		125
(5) turnover of a leading agency, index	n.a.	100	144		230

*The 1967 figure apparently excludes radio and television advertising. See the table 8.5. The growth between 1967 and 1968 is also affected by rises of about 30 per cent in advertising rates.

per annum.[9] The available figures, however, do not clearly confirm that this has happened.

For principal media advertising only (rows (1) and (2)), there certainly have been very rapid increases, even allowing for the rate rises of 1968. However, this growth, according to these estimates, has slowed. (The first half 1970 figures were in fact 18 per cent up on first half 1969, according to Dr Ravasz.) The agency turnover index (row (5)) also suggests very rapid growth in media bookings, though of course it is no adequate measure of the overall rate of growth.[10] However, if series for display advertising alone were available for the USSR and Poland they might show similar growth, since media advertising has grown faster there, too, than total advertising. The estimate for total advertising (rows (3) and (4)) shows an increase between 1969 and 1970 apparently of a Russo-Polish order.

However, the non-media (approximately 'below-the-line') component of both the A and B estimates is avowedly very

[9] By analogy with the growth rates of UK advertising expenditure in the early post-war period.
[10] Because the agency in question may well have increased its share in total business (primarily at the expense of billings not channelled through agencies).

much a guesstimate, and perhaps the guesses about it have not been revised upwards as sharply of late as they should have been. At this point the figures are not reliable enough to support or refute an *ex-post* prediction of explosive growth in total advertising expenditure.

For media composition the estimates by Dr Ravasz, obtained directly from the media, are shown in table 8.5.

TABLE 8.5   Estimated media breakdown, Hungarian advertising, 1967—9 inclusive (m. forints)

	1967	1968	1969	percentage shares 1969 of principal media total	of grand total
press	82.2	169.1	218.0	83.4	21.8
radio	**	2.7	8.9	3.4	0.9
television	**	4.1	12.5	4.8	1.3
cinema	3.7	4.5	5.6	2.1	0.6
transport	5.4	6.9	5.5	2.1	0.6
posters*	7.0	9.4	10.9	4.2	1.1
total of above	98.3†	196.7	261.4	100	26.1
other advertising and promotion	n.a.	n.a.	c.740		74
grand total	n.a.	n.a.	c.1000		100

*other than transport
**negligible
†excluding radio and television

Press advertising here includes classified advertisements. Some production and administrative costs are distributed among the media headings. Dr Ravasz considers the individual principal media items to have a margin of error of ± 10 per cent, except for the item 'press', where only incomplete data were obtainable from the media. The 'other advertising and promotion' for 1969 is a guesstimate based, I gather, on the assumption that expenditure on exhibitions and printed promotional matter is equivalent to the same percentage of GNP as in West European countries. In other words, it is highly problematic but not implausible.

Another estimate, which I have made on the basis of
major-agency turnover data and some agency judgements of
their share in total advertising under each heading, comes out
as follows for 1970 (m. forints):

printed promotional matter	300—420
press	*c.*250
television	*c.*15
transport	*c.*16

No estimates of the product-group composition of total
advertising expenditure are available. Classified advertising is
included in the press totals quoted above and probably
accounts for a larger proportion of press advertising expenditure than in the UK.[11] Data on the relative importance of
producer goods advertising are lacking. It appears to be of
some importance in principal media expenditure, and in the
opinion of some specialists may account for a larger share of
media advertising expenditure than in Western Europe, as
well as for a substantial part of total national 'below-the-line'
promotional spending.

Yugoslavia
There are several estimates of Yugoslav advertising expenditure but they are all dubious. They differ widely. Some
specialists believe their own estimates are about right, but
hardly anyone seems ready to accept anyone else's estimate.
The intended coverage is always wide, including a large
below-the-line element. But the actual coverage is always very
uncertain.
      Up to 1965 there were official figures derived from
enterprise financial reporting, but they have no credibility
among advertising practitioners and academic marketing
specialists.[12] A study by Jovanovic and others, based on a

---

[11] Judging by casual inspection of newspapers only.
[12] For the sort of reasons given in the article by Dr F. Rocco in the
journal of The Yugoslav Marketing Association, *Marketing* (Zagreb,
1971), no. 1, *plus* the fact that in pre-1965 conditions there was greater
pressure 'from above' on enterprises which might lead to deliberate
distortion of information 'from below'.

questionnaire survey, apparently of advertisers rather than media, was described in a 1969 article.[13] It is clearly the most systematic attempt so far to get reliable figures, but it is generally believed to yield totals that are too low. The reason for this, it is said, is that enterprises reported unrealistically low advertising appropriations, either deliberately or because their own accounting gave incomplete figures. Jovanovic's article unfortunately does not give details of definitions and methods used. ZIT, probably the leading market research organisation, is beginning to assemble total advertising expenditure estimates by making periodic censuses of press advertising space and television and radio time, etc., and applying the appropriate rates to them to yield expenditure figures. ZIT staff consider that advertisers' and media accounts are not capable of yielding reliable and consistently defined data to questionnaire surveys.

TABLE 8.6   Estimates of total advertising expenditure in Yugoslavia, various years (m. new dinars)

	1968	1969	1970	1970—71	1971
Jovanovic	375	459*	(562)**		
Loncar		900	1200		
guesstimate A			750		
guesstimate B				600	1500†

*forecast by Jovanovic *et al.*
**extrapolation by the present author from Jovanovic's 1969 forecast; the percentage increase in the 1969 forecast over 1968 (22.4) was applied to the 1969 forecast figure to give a hypothetical 1970 total.
†forecast by Loncar.
Sources: Jovanovic: Milan R. Jovanovic, 'Koliko se u Jugoslaviji trosi za ekonomsku propagandu' ('How Much is Spent on Economic Propaganda in Yugoslavia'), *Direktor* (Belgrade, April 1969) p. 78.
Loncar: private communication from Dr F. Rocco of ZIT.

The estimates of Loncar (see table 8.6) are thought to be too high. They are apparently a scaling-up of data from a small and probably unrepresentative sample of advertisers. From discussions with staff of the market research organisation ZIT and of the OZEHA advertising agency I have

[13] M. R. Jovanovic, 'Koliko se u Jugoslaviji trosi za ekonomsku propagandu' ('How much is spent on economic propaganda in Yugoslavia'), *Direktor* (Belgrade, April 1969).

added a couple of guesstimates of my own from partial data (e.g. total press advertising in one week, total agency turnover) plus specialists' opinions as to the relative importance of these partial data in total expenditure. The various figures that are available in these various ways are given in table 8.6. In principle, the Jovanovic data cover media advertising *plus* printed promotional matter *plus* fairs and exhibitions *plus* free gifts and samples. Whether they are intended to include some point-of-sale (e.g. shop-window display) expenditure and packaging costs is not clear. Loncar's precise intended coverage is not known to me. Guesstimates A and B exclude all point-of-sale and packaging. Advertising by foreign concerns is generally included, at least in principle.

For estimates of the rate of growth of advertising expenditure the only plausible series known to me is the Jovanonic series. If his figures for any one year are in fact too low, it does not of course follow that the time series understates the growth rate. On the other hand it is not clear from the article whether we have any reason to expect that any degree of understatement that existed was consistent from year to year. With these crippling provisos, the figures are given in table 8.7.

TABLE 8.7   Yugoslav advertising expenditure, percentage increase over previous year, 1962—9

1962	1963	1964	1965	1966	1967	1968	(1969)
30.0	15.4	12.5	19.4	12.1	24.8	24.2	(22.4)

Source: derived from Jovanovic, *Direktor* (April 1969) p. 78.

If these rates of increase are approximately right, they are moderately comforting (and if not, not). They show an acceleration in spending on advertising after the 1965 reforms which supports our primitive hypothesis that a socialist economy that substantially increases its use of the market mechanism will experience just such an acceleration in marketing expenditure.[14]

[14] See Section 3 (on Hungary) and the conclusions of chapter 4.

The acceleration, if real, was more marked than the figures suggest at first sight. The Yugoslav economy has had greater fluctuations in its growth over the past decade, in real terms, and also very much greater price variations, than the Polish, Hungarian or Soviet economies. This is relevant here. The rates of increase shown here from 1966 to 1968 occurred in a period when both real output and price increases were less than in 1960—6. The national income price deflator, 1960=100, rose to 220 in 1966 but only to 229 by 1968.[15] The official retail price index (1968=100) also more than doubled (43 to 90) from 1960 to 1966 and grew more slowly for the next two years, by a further 11 per cent.[16] 'Real' (1960 prices) net material product rose 56 per cent from 1960 to 1966, but only another 6 per cent through 1968.[17] Therefore the acceleration of advertising expenditure from 1966 onwards almost certainly represents a much sharper increase in the share of national resources being used in advertising than the increases in such spending at current prices, in isolation, would suggest.[18]

On the other hand, the rates of increase from 1966 on, according to the Jovanovic series, are not clearly greater than the apparent rates of increase revealed by the (admittedly very sketchy) Soviet and Polish data. More will be said on this point below.

The relative importance of different media in Yugoslavia is something on which there are fewer data than on total advertising expenditure. From what data there are, however, one obtains a very plausible picture of a shift away from a roughly Soviet-style mix at the beginning of the 1960s, with a sharply increasing share going to media advertising in general and to television, radio and press in particular.

Jovanovic gives a broad advertising and promotion-mix and

[15] Derived from official series of net material product in 1960 and in current prices, *Statisticki godisnjak Jugoslavije 1970 (Statistical Year-book of Yugoslavia 1970)* (Belgrade, 1970) pp. 100 and 102 respectively.

[16] ibid. p. 259.

[17] ibid. p. 100.

[18] Since there is no reason to suppose that changes in the relative prices of goods and services used in advertising, compared with other prices, were sufficient to yield an opposite result. They would have had to be very large to do so.

TABLE 8.8   Advertising and promotion expenditure in Yugoslavia by
             major categories, 1961, 1965, 1968 and forecast 1969
             (m. new dinars)

	1961	1965	1968	forecast 1969
advertisements*	9	30	65	80
fairs and exhibitions	38	64	90	90
printed matter	25	54	84	140
other†	48	27	136	148
	100	215	375	459

*This is literally translated. It appears to mean 'display advertising'.
†It appears from the text that this includes bonus offers, point-of-sale
advertising and promotional competitions. It may include other items
as well.
Source: Jovanovic, *Direktor*, (April 1969) p. 78.

a breakdown by principal media, from which the following
material (tables 8.8 and 8.9) are taken. Once more, it cannot
be assumed that this is an accurate picture. It is widely
believed that the total is too small, and it is not clear that the
relative shares of different media and promotional methods
need be right, even with quite a wide margin of error.

The exact meaning of the figures in table 8.9 is not
entirely clear from the text, but they appear to be shares in
total display advertising. 'Press' probably includes relatively
little classified (small) advertising, and may exclude it
altogether. Whether poster, transport and neon advertising is
included is not clear.

TABLE 8.9   Percentage shares of principal media in advertising
             expenditure in Yugoslavia, late 1960s*

daily newspapers	24
specialist periodicals	14
radio	18
television	22
'publications'	13
other	9
	100

*Approximately, shares in total display advertising. The period referred
to is probably 1968.
Source: Jovanovic, *Direktor* (April 1969) p. 79.

If the above interpretation of table 8.9 is correct, tables 8.8 and 8.9· taken together imply that in 1968 television accounted for only about 4 per cent of total advertising and promotional expenditure. The approximately equivalent figure for the UK would be 16 per cent. For newspapers the Yugoslav share in total spending likewise appears to be 4 per cent whereas for the UK the corresponding percentage would be about 23.[19] Thus the Yugoslav pattern of advertising and promotional expenditure in 1968 was still heavily slanted towards exhibitions, catalogues, leaflets and similar below -the-line methods; and television and mass-circulation press advertising, though it had risen fast, was still relatively less important than in the UK — according to the Jovanovic figures. If these comparisons are very broadly right — as they would seem from casual observation to be — the Yugoslav 'marketing mix' is still quite 'old-fashioned' and has some way to go before it approaches current West European patterns. This helps to explain the proposals for establishing a second, entirely commercially-sponsored television channel in Zagreb, for example. In the present Yugoslav economic system a further, very rapid, expansion of mass-media advertising is very likely, provided balance-of-payments and inflationary problems do not lead either to very drastic deflationary policies or to a substantial return to administrative controls on the economy. Jovanovic and his colleagues project a quadrupling of display advertising expenditure between 1968 and 1975,[20] and no doubt expect the television share of this total to rise if present time, channel and production capacity constraints are loosened.

For estimates of the product-mix of Yugoslav advertising, Jovanovic is again the only source. And again there must be doubts about the accuracy of the figures. Jovanovic gives two tables that are of particular interest. One is a breakdown of the total advertising and promotion expenditure by economic branch. The other shows estimated advertising and promotion expenditure as a percentage of sales for a number of

---

[19] 'Advertising Expenditure 1964—1968' (Advertising Association survey data), supplement to *Advertising Quarterly* (Summer 1969).
[20] Jovanovic, *Direktor* (April 1969).

TABLE 8.10   Economic-branch breakdown of estimated advertising
and promotion expenditure in Yugoslavia, 1961, 1965,
1968 and forecast 1969 (m. new dinars)

branch	1961	1965	1968	forecast 1969
engineering	24.1	41.0	60.3	70
iron and steel	8.3	12.0	22.0	30
electrical equipment	12.1	25.5	50.0	70
food	11.0	28.5	58.7	60
textiles	8.8	21.4	49.0	55
agriculture, forestry, woodworking	9.8	20.6	31.0	40
coal	4.3	12.4	11.9	9
construction	3.3	11.5	12.0	20
trade	6.0	20.4	48.4	60
transport	3.8	11.6	14.3	20
cultural-social activities	1.8	4.8	12.4	25
other	6.6	5.3	5.0	10
total	100.0	215.0	375.0	459

Source: Jovanovic, *Direktor* (April 1969).

product groups, compared with corresponding figures for US
product groups. These tables are given here in part tables
8.10 and 8.11.

Tables 8.10 and 8.11 suggest that the initiative in incurring
advertising expenditure is fairly widely spread in the Yugoslav economy, though such expenditure is probably not of
West European or North American importance (relatively to
production) in any one branch. (It must also be borne in
mind that this is spending with a large share of non-media
promotional activity, and that display advertising alone may
be very differently distributed between branches and will
generally be much smaller).

Whereas in the Soviet-type economy marketing activities,
and hence advertising, tend to be confined to the distributive
system and a few producers faced with buyers' markets, in
the Yugoslav figures given here trade apparently accounted
for only 6 per cent of expenditure in 1961 and 13 per cent in
1968 (not far from the Kaldor-Silverman figure for UK 1938:
10 per cent).[21]

[21] See Harris and Seldon, *Advertising and the Public*, p. 44.

TABLE 8.11 Advertising and promotion expenditure as percentage of
sales, certain product groups, Yugoslavia and USA, 1961
and 1967*

product group	Yugoslavia		USA	
	1961	1967	1961	1967
motor vehicles	0.5	1.0	1.9	8.9
household appliances	0.3	2.0	7.9	18.3
radio & television equipment	0.9	2.1	2.5	11.1
oil products	0.1	1.2	0.7	0.9
soap and detergents	0.5	3.0	13.2	22.5
cosmetics	0.8	2.0	9.1	24.5
drinks	0.9	1.5	3.9	7.8
tobacco	0.1	1.0	3.7	8.6
food	0.8	2.0	2.1	3.9
confectionery	1.3	1.2	4.0	14.5
rubber products	0.1	0.5	1.6	1.9

*I infer these dates from the text, which describes the table as being
'for the period 1961—1967' and then gives two columns of figures for
each country. I have not found the US source (which Jovanovic does
not give). The 1961 US percentages are close, where comparable, to
those given by Harris and Seldon in *Advertising and the Public* p. 55,
for USA 1959. The latter figures were derived from *Printers' Ink*,
Fortune and *Advertising Age*. 'Sales' here appears to mean company
sales at wholesale prices.
Source: Jovanovic, *Direktor* (April 1969) p. 79.

The branch-distribution of expenditure in 1968 is not very
different from 1961. The only percentage shares which are
more than three points different in 1968 are food, textiles
and trade (up) and engineering and 'other' (down).

Table 8.11 must be read, as Jovanovic points out, with the
relatively low output levels of the Yugoslav economy in
mind. This means that advertising budgets are very small —
smaller than even a casual glance at the percentages
suggests. He also gives, from his survey data, ranges for
typical annual advertising budgets of large enterprises, for
some economic branches, in new dinars, as follows:

engineering	1000—2500	textiles	900—2400
electrical equipment	1500—4000	food industry	800—6000
chemical industry	800—9000	distribution	200—1500
woodworking	600—1800		

Thus, of course, advertising and promotional expenditure
in major branches of the Yugoslav economy in the late 1960s
was not only generally of lower relative importance than for
the equivalent US branches in the early 1960s, but in any direct
firm-by-firm comparison would appear minuscule in absolute
value terms. Since the output of the Yugoslav economy is not
much larger than that of General Motors, however, and there
are over two and a half thousand Yugoslav industrial

TABLE 8.12 Estimated advertising expenditure and total household
consumption expenditure, Poland, Hungary and
Yugoslavia, 1968 or 1969 (current prices)

	(1) advertising expenditure		(2) household consumption	(3) (1) as % of (2)
	minimum	maximum		
Poland (milliard zlotys, 1968)	0.45*	1.05*	429.7	0.1—0.2
Hungary (milliard forints, 1969)	1.00	1.02	157**	0.6—0.8
Yugoslavia (m. new dinars, 1969)	459	900	57,000†	0.8—1.6

*obtained by applying the ratios (rounded) of the minimum and
maximum plausible estimates for 1970 (see text above) to the official
returns for 1970 to the official returns for 1968.
**net personal material consumption only (approximate).
†Approximate. Obtained by reducing the official figure for total
personal net incomes by the average percentage discrepancy between
household income and consumption from household budget survey
data in 1968 (discrepancy = recording error + personal savings).
Samples for budget surveys are not representative of the whole
population.
Sources: For advertising data, see text above. For consumption data:
Poland: *Kratkii statisticheskii yezhegodnik PNR 1970*) (*Short statistical
Yearbook of Poland, 1970*) (Warsaw, 1970) pp. 18 (population) and
345 (personal consumption per head of population); Hungary: (Hungarian) Central Statistical Office, *Hungary Today* (Budapest, 1970) pp.
166 (approx. personal per material consumption per capita) and inside
cover (population); Yugoslavia: *Statisticki Kalendar Jugoslavije 1971*,
(Belgrade, 1971) pp. 47 (total personal income), 96 and 97 (household
budget data).

enterprises,[22] it would be unreasonable to expect anything else. The Yugoslav proponents of increased advertising expenditure who bewail the fact that a medium-sized (in US terms) US company may spend more on advertising than the whole of the corresponding branch of Yugoslav industry are playing fast and loose with the arithmetical possibilities.

Systematic estimates of the relative importance of classified, consumer-goods and producer-goods advertising are lacking.

Comparisons of expenditure
This final sub-section on advertising expenditure deals only with the totals, and offers some tentative international comparisons. With the provisos noted above, the most useful method of comparison is to express the estimated expenditure as a percentage of total household consumer expenditure. The resulting percentages give a rough idea of the relative importance of advertising in each country. The differences in the coverage of the different national advertising data are not very great in principle, but they may well be large in practice (see above).

Table 8.12 gives plausible ranges of advertising and promotion expenditure and relates them to total household consumption spending.

[22] Statisticki Kalendar Jugoslavije 1971 *(Statistical Calendar of Yugoslavia 1971)* (Belgrade, 1971) p. 65.

Part II: Conclusions

Part III Conclusions

9 Conclusions

Table 8.12 provides a starting-point for considering the significance of advertising in the Soviet Union and Eastern Europe, compared with its role in the West. If we add percentages roughly comparable with those in the last column of that table for the UK, USSR and Czechoslovakia, we get the following picture.

TABLE 9.1   Estimated advertising expenditure as percentage of total household consumption, 1967, 1968, 1969

USSR 1967	Poland 1969	Hungary 1969	Czechoslovakia 1967	Yugoslavia 1969	UK 1968
0.03—0.07	0.1—0.2	0.6—0.8	0.1—0.3*	0.8—1.6	2.9—3.3†

*percentages of total personal material consumption.
†media advertising estimates (Advertising Association) *plus* an estimated £300—400 million of 'below-the-line' promotional expenditure.
Sources: USSR: *The Development of Advertising in the Soviet Union*, p. 17; Poland, Hungary, Yugoslavia: table 8.12; UK: *Advertising Association, Advertising Expenditure 1964—1968*, supplement to *The Advertising Quarterly* (Summer 1969), and *The Times* (14 May 1970) p. 25; Czechoslovakia: Advertising expenditure from a guide to marketing in Eastern Europe by Mr J. R. Mikton of UNCTAD/GATT (privately communicated). Consumption total from official statistical yearbook, *Statisticka rocenka CSSR 1969* (Prague, 1969) p. 151.

It is obvious from all that has been said so far that these comparative percentages rest (except for the UK) on the shakiest statistical foundations. Hence the use of ranges of probably estimates. The orders of magnitude seem *a priori* about right, but if they did not I should prefer my *a priori* expectations to this empirical evidence.

What, if anything, do they suggest? They must be considered with relative national GNP and consumption levels (appendix 1 to chaper 5) in mind. I conclude, first, that advertising expenditure in these socialist countries is relatively smaller than in Britain; second, that in the two countries practising forms of market socialism — Hungary and Yugo-slavia — the importance of advertising is markedly higher than in the countries with detailed administrative planning; third, that this difference is due to their having a more market-oriented form of socialism, rather than to their income levels, which if anything would tend to work in the opposite direction (contrast Yugoslavia and Czechoslovakia). If there were similar reforms in other Comecon countries they should produce a similar growth of advertising.

Fourth, Hungary and Yugoslavia show markedly less advertising and promotion activity (relatively) than does the UK. However, (and fifth), considering their income levels, the limited time they have so far had at playing with markets, the recent growth of advertising expenditure and forecasts of future development, I would expect these percentages to increase. There is however a danger of exaggerating the extent to which they have 'gone over' to being 'market' economies. As was pointed out in chapter 6, they retain strong central control by West European standards (especially Hungary). From this comes my final conclusion: it does not follow that advertising should become as important, in this particular numerical sense, as it is in the UK at present — it might or it might not.

The growth rates of advertising expenditure in these countries might also be considered. It was not clear that they were higher in Hungary or Yugoslavia than in the USSR and Poland. Does this mean that the distinction between market and administrative socialist economies is not really so important after all? Hardly, for apart from the sketchiness of the data, these growth rates will be substantially affected by many things; for example, the initial levels and concurrent growth rates of real GNP and personal incomes; the general price level and changes in price structure; the rate at which sellers' markets are being ended, and how large they are; media and other capacity constraints; the initial level of advertising activity; the extent to which the role of the market mechanism is being increased (rather than the extent of its use in any one short period of time).

British advertising expenditure grew extremely fast in a post-war period of de-control that was in some ways similar to the decentralisation of a Soviet-type economy. But such growth has the special rapidity of a recovery process. In economies that have been administratively controlled for a substantial time, are experimenting with new forms of organisation and have never had a 'developed' marketing system, shortages of capacity (including skilled specialists) may be an important constraint. Perhaps explosive growth in total advertising and promotion expenditure (of over 30 per cent p.a., say) is not to be expected, though in media display advertising alone it is more likely.

There is not a great deal to be added to the conclusions already given in earlier chapters (especially chapter 4). The broad questions that have been raised are, first, what role can there be for commercial advertising in a socialist economy? and second, what lessons may be learned from East European experience about the role of advertising in capitalist countries?

If the East European economies are socialist, then commercial advertising is not incompatible with socialism. In all of them it is treated as a necessary and useful technique. Its ultimate rationale is that it helps to raise material consumption levels and that the raising of material consumption levels is desirable.

State and co-operative enterprises in Eastern Europe have tended to find increasing incentives to advertise and, generally, to incur marketing expenditure for consumer goods. This seems to be the result in all cases of an easing of sellers' markets associated with a rise in consumption levels and hence in discretionary consumer spending.

The volume of advertising relative to private consumption in general or to sales of particular product groups, remains well below West European levels. However, there is a fairly clear difference between those economies that retain broadly Soviet-type administrative control and those that have developed forms of market socialism. In the first case advertising remains far less developed than in the West. There are reasons for expecting it to develop further as incomes rise, but is doubtful whether it will develop anything approaching Western levels and patterns as long as the centralised administrative economic system is retained.

Hungary and Yugoslavia have more Western patterns of

advertising expenditure and organisation and of incentives to advertise, and the functions of advertising generally do not seem to differ in kind from those observable in Western Europe. However, certain constraints on the total levels of media advertising, on the sorts of advertising message acceptable and perhaps (though this is very uncertain) on heavy 'defensive' (mutually cancelling brand-competitive) advertising seem still to exist in Hungary and may be retained. In Yugoslavia such controls are less evident.

I conclude that substantial consumer advertising, being a form of marketing, is a corollary of a market economy, with or without private ownership of resources. It is not self-evident that it needs to be as substantial in a market socialist economy as in Western Europe or North America, but it may be that the benefits of competition and the market mechanism in micro-economic decision-making in a large part of the economy cannot be obtained without allowing substantial advertising expenditure, and that advertising cannot be held much below 'Western' levels without losing some of those benefits. From this, as from many points of view, the Hungarian economy especially is going to be interesting to watch.

None of this proves that advertising arrangements elsewhere are wonderful or that those who are critical of Western mass consumption society should look at, for example, Soviet society and forget their complaints. Fortunately, there is no existing set of social arrangements that cannot be improved on. What the experience of the socialist countries does support is the view that marketing activities have social merits closely bound up with the advantages long claimed by writers in the liberal tradition for markets and market relations in general.

The guided market systems of Hungary and Yugoslavia are attempts, subject to great political and economic difficulties, to operate socialist economies without following the Soviet centralised, administrative model. Nobody can say for certain that highly centralised economic control must sooner or later entail highly centralised social and political control, or that economic decentralisation must lead to greater political freedom. All the same, political and economic relationships are peculiarly hard to separate in Soviet-type systems, and the domestic political record of modern states with centralised peacetime economies is pretty nasty.

The civil rights kind of dissent among Soviet intellectuals is one response to Soviet centralism. What we might call acquisitive dissent is another. In all the Socialist countries consumer grumbles exert a strong long-run pressure towards more market-oriented economic arrangements. Meanwhile, the passionate pursuit of Western consumer goods by many young Russians suggests that one needs to live in a Western consumer society to see its defects and in Russia, perhaps, to see its charms.

Appendix A

Bibliography of Soviet publications cited in Part I

Books
  (1) D. B. Bekleshov, *Reklama v promyshlennosti* (*Advertising in industry*) (Moscow, 1969).
  (2) D. B. Bekleshov, and K. G. Voronov, *Reklama v torgovle* (*Advertising in trade*) (Moscow, 1968).
  (3) N. M. Bogacheva, and M. Zubovich, *Bibliograficheskii ukazatel literatury po reklame* (*Advertising bibliography*) (Moscow, 1969).
  (4) N. I. Buzlyakov, *Metody planirovaniya povysshenia urovnya zhizni* (*Methods of planning the raising of living standards*) (Moscow, 1969).
  (5) Yu. Degtyarev, and L. Kornilov, *Torgovaya reklama: ekonomika, iskusstvo* (*Trade advertising: economics, art*) (Moscow, 1969).
  (6) I. I. Gol'tsekker, and Yu. N. Khachaturov, *Torgovaya reklama v potrebitelskoi kooperatsii* (*Trade advertising in the consumer cooperative society*) (Moscow, 1969).
  (7) A. L. Vainshtein, *Narodnyi dokhod Rossii i SSSR* (*National income of Russia and the USSR*) (Moscow, 1969).
  (8) (collective authors), *Ekonomicheskaya reforma i sovershentstvovanie torgovli (The economic reform and the improvement of trade*) (Moscow, 1969).
  (9a) (RSFSR Ministry of Trade, Rostorgreklama), *Organizatsiya i tekhnika reklamy tekhnicheskii listok no. 3 (Organisation and technique of advertising, technical booklet no. 3*) (Moscow, 1969).
  (9b) (RSFSR Ministry of Trade, Rostorgreklama), *Organizatsiya i tekhnika reklamy tekhnicheskii listok no. 4* (Moscow, 1969).

Articles
Key: EG *Ekonomicheskaya Gazeta (Economic Gazette)*, weekly
      PKh *Planovoe Khozyaistvo (Planned Economy)*, monthly
      ST *Sovetskaya Torgovlya (Soviet Trade)*, monthly
      P   *Pravda*
      I   *Izvestiya*
      LG *Literaturnaya Gazeta (Literary Gazette)*, weekly
  (10) M. Artemova, 'O fonde potrebleniya v natsional 'nom dokhode' ('On the consumption fund in national income'), *PKh*, (1969) no. 12, pp. 45—50.

(11) A. Bachurin, 'V. I. Lenin i sovremennye problemy planirovaniya narodnogo khozyaistva' ('V. I. Lenin and contemporary problems of economic planning), *PKh.*, (1969), no. 11, pp. 3—19.

(12) V. Bugaev, 'Effektivnye formy reklamnoi raboty' ('Effective forms of advertising work'), *ST* (1969) no. 2, pp. 50—3.

(13) E. Chernyak and V. Bogoraz, 'Obsluzhivaet avtomat' ('The automatic vending machine serves [the Customer]), *P* (10 May 1970).

(14) Yu. Degtyarev and L. Kornilov, 'Auktsion — raz, auktsion — dva, auktsion — tri!' ('Going, going, gone!'), *Nedelya* (Sunday supplement to *I*) (3 April 1969).

(15) A. Grebnev and I. Rybchenko, 'Ekonomiko-matematicheskie metody v planirovanii tovarooborota' ('Mathematical-economic methods in planning retail turnover'), *PKh* (1969) no. 1, pp. 20—31.

(16) I. Ivanova, 'Izuchenie sprosa posredstvom anket' ('Market research by means of questionnaires'), *ST* (1968) no. 1, pp. 23—5.

(17) Ye. Kanevskii, 'Reklama vo ves' rost' ('All-out Growth for Advertising'), *I* (2 April 1969).

(18) Ye. Kanevskii, 'Svistok sud'i i molotok auktsionera' ('The referee's whistle and the auctioneer's hammer'), *ST* (1969) no. 10, pp. 53—6.

(19) Ye. Kedrin and Ye. Darinskaya, 'Vyborochnyne nablyudeniya za realizatsiei obuvi' ('Sample observations on footwear sales'), *ST* (1970) no. 2, pp. 36—9.

(20) F. Krutikov and B. Sobol'ev 'Opredeleniye potrebnosti v tovarakh dlitel' nogo pol zovaniys' ('The determination of requirements for consumer durables'), *ST* (1969) no. 2, pp. 25—9.

(21) V. Mayevskii, 'Narodnokhozyaistvennyi optimum i planirovanie struktury potrebleniya' ('The national economic optimum and the planning of the structure of consumption'), *PKh* (1969) no. 1, pp. 20—31.

(22) A. Markushevich, 'Psikhologicheskoe vozdeistvie reklamy' ('The psychological impact of advertising'), *ST* (1968) no. 9, pp. 57—61.

(23) A. Nastenko, 'Reklama, kakoi yei byt'? ('What sort of advertising'?), *EG* (1969) no. 28, p. 11.

(24) L. Opatskii, 'Uluchshenie struktury otraslei vtorogo podrazdeleniya' ('Improving the structures of branches in sector II'), *PKh* (1969) no. 12, pp. 45—50.

(25) L. Ostrovskii, 'Chto skazali 4000 pokupateli' ('What 4000 customers said'), *ST* (1969) no. 3, pp. 27—9.

(26) L. Ostrovskii, O. Kostko and I. Kochneva, 'Shirokii assortiment i neudovletvorennyi spros' ('Wide assortment and unsatisfied demand'), *ST* (1970) no. 1, pp. 28—9.

(27) V. Rusakova, and G. Studets, 'Vspomnim o reklame' ('Let's remember advertising'), *P* (19 February 1969).

(28) F. Sagitdinov, 'Pri pomoshchi anket' ('With the help of quest-
     ionnaires'), *ST* (1969) no. 2, pp. 25—9.
(29) S. Sarukhanov, 'Reklame — slovo' ('A word on advertising'), *ST*
     (1969) no. 8 pp. 51—5.
(30) V. Sarykulova, 'Kritika kontseptsii detsentralizatsii ekonomiki'
     ('A critique of concepts of economic decentralisation'), *PKh*
     (1969) no. 12, pp. 27—36.
(31) R. Sorokina, 'Organizatsiya reklamnykh kampanii', ('The
     organisation of advertising campaigns'), *ST* (1969) no. 3, pp.
     54—7.
(32) M. Tadzhibaev, 'Statisticheskoe izuchenie rynka obuvi' ('Statis-
     tical research on the footwear market'), *ST* (1970) no. 1, pp.
     24—8.
(33) V. A. Trapeznikov, '"Glagoli" upravleniya: znayet, mozhet,
     khochet, uspevaet' ('The management "verbs": knows, can,
     wants, succeeds'), *LG* (13 May 1970).
(34) V. Usov, 'Kat "Odevat" konditerskiye izdeliya' ('How to "clothe"
     confectionary'), *ST* (1968) no. 8, pp. 41—3.
(35) V. Varavka, 'Trud prodavtsa' ('The sales assistant's labour'), *EG*
     (1970) no. 19, p. 17.
(36) V. Volodeeva and V. Solov'ev, 'Organizatsii reklamnoi kampanii
     po syram' ('The organisation of an advertising campaign for
     cheese'), *ST* (1969) no. 9, pp. 49—51.
(37) A. Yermakov, 'Komu vygodna reklama?' ('Who benefits from
     advertising?'), *Zhurnalist (Journalist)* (1968) no. 5, p. 42, and
     anonymous article, *ibid.*, p. 43.
(38) V. Yurov, 'Zakazy i stimuli ikh vypol'neniya', ('Orders and
     incentives to fulfil them'), *ST* (1970) no. 2, pp. 10—13.

Statistical Handbooks
(39) Tsentral'noe statisticheskoe upravlenie, *Narodnoe khozyaistvo
     SSSR v 1968 g.* (Central Statistical Administration, *The National
     Economy of the USSR in 1968*) (Moscow, 1969).

Appendix B

1. What was total national advertising expenditure in the most recent year for which data are available? . . . .

2. What was total advertising expenditure in each of any of the five preceding years for which data are available? . . . .

3. (*a*) Which of the following kinds of advertising expenditure are included in the above data?
(*b*) If a breakdown of total expenditure between some or all of these headings is available for a recent year (preferably the most recent), please give it.

		(tick box if included in 1 above)	expenditure	year
(*a*)	shop-window display	☐	. . . .	. . . .
(*b*)	outdoor (billboards, neon signs)	☐	. . . .	. . . . .
(*c*)	catalogues, brochures, leaflets	☐	. . . .	. . . . .
(*d*)	press advertising	☐	. . . .	. . . . .
(*e*)	cinema advertising	☐	. . . .	. . . . .
(*f*)	television advertising	☐	. . . .	. . . . .
(*g*)	radio advertising	☐	. . . .	. . . . .
(*h*)	exhibitions	☐	. . . .	. . . . .
(*i*)	free gifts and samples	☐	. . . .	. . . . .
(*j*)	any other (please indicate which)	☐	. . . .	. . . . .

4. How reliable do you personally consider the above data to be?

(Tick where appropriate)

5. Where a media-breakdown is available, are the costs of (*a*) the administration of advertising and (*b*) production (blocks, film

production etc) allocated between
the various media headings, or are
they treated separately?

| (*a*) Admin included under other headings ☐ | (*b*) Prod costs included under other headings ☐ |
| separate ☐ | separate ☐ |

(Tick the appropriate box)

6. Are the major specialised advertising
organisations
   (*a*) subordinate to the Ministries of   ☐
   Internal and Foreign Trade only?
   (*b*) subordinate to Internal Trade,   ☐
   Foreign Trade and Production
   Ministries?
   (*c*) not subordinate to any branch   ☐
   ministry?

7. Would you say that it was usual for
enterprises manufacturing consumer
goods to have their own advertising sections?

(Tick the appropriate box)

8. Is domestic advertising expenditure
   (*a*)   initiated and financed mainly
           by internal trade organisations?   ☐
   (*b*)   initiated mainly by internal
           trade organisations but with
           producing enterprises or
           ministries taking an
           approximately equal share of
           financial burden?   ☐
   (*c*)   initiated and financed in
           approximately equal degrees
           by internal trade and
           producing organisations?   ☐
   (*d*)   initiated and financed mainly
           by producing organisations?   ☐
   (*e*)   initiated and financed in some
           other way? (please specify)   ☐

9. Are any data available on the
breakdown of advertising
expenditure by product group (e.g.
food and non-food; food, consumer
durables, other manufactured
consumer goods, or more detailed

breakdowns)? If so, can you give this breakdown for any recent year, or supply a reference to a source where it may be found?

10. Are any data available on the breakdown of advertising expenditure between personal (classified), consumer-goods and producer-goods advertising?

Index of Authors

Index of Subjects